TALKING POINTS IN PSYCHOLOGY

TUTORIAL TOPICS FOR STUDENTS AND TEACHERS

Rob McIlveen

Martyn Long

Anthony Curtis

Hodder & Stoughton

A MEMBER OF THE HODDER HEADLINE GROUP

DEDICATION

To Gill, Katie and William

British Library Cataloguing in Publication Data

A catalogue for this title is available from the British Library

ISBN 0 340 60647 9

First published 1994
Impression number   10 9 8 7 6 5 4 3 2 1
Year   1999 1998 1997 1996 1995 1994

Typeset by Wearset, Boldon, Tyne and Wear.
Printed in Great Britain for Hodder & Stoughton Educational, a division of Hodder Headline Plc, 338 Euston Road, London NW1 3BH by St Edmundsbury Press, Bury St Edmunds, Suffolk.

Contents

Preface

Our aim in writing this book was to produce something that would encourage students to think more critically about aspects of psychology they are likely to encounter in pre-degree, degree, and general interest courses. In this book, we offer 10 topics that could form the basis either for classroom discussion or individual or small group tutorial sessions. The topics we have chosen have been selected to cover a wide variety of areas of psychological concern. These include biological psychology, cognitive psychology, social psychology, developmental psychology, abnormal psychology, comparative psychology and individual differences.

Each chapter begins with what can be described as a 'target article'. The target articles have been taken from both broadsheet and tabloid British newspapers. In some cases, the articles are written by an author actively involved in the area the article addresses. In other cases, the articles have been written by journalists. Whichever, the target articles are, we feel, ones which are likely to be of interest to both students and teachers of psychology at any level.

The target article in Chapter one addresses the issues of the determinants of handedness. Chapter two's target article adopts a critical approach to multiple personality disorder. In Chapter three, the target article considers the provocative question of what determines homosexuality. Chapter four's target article examines the relative contribution of 'nature' and 'nurture' to the development of psychological characteristics. In Chapter five, the target article is an obituary of B.F. Skinner, written from a critical perspective. The target article in Chapter six offers arguments for the use of electroconvulsive therapy in the treatment of mental disorders. In Chapter seven, the target article considers some of the implications of forename stereotyping. The target article in Chapter eight addresses issues concerning morality. Chapter nine's target article examines dental phobia and the methods that are available to treat the dentally phobic. Finally, in Chapter ten, the target article describes the events at the first world memory championship, and considers how incredible feats of memory are achieved.

Following each target article, we present background information relevant to the topic addressed. In some, perhaps all, of the chapters, teachers of psychology will be thoroughly familiar with the area addressed by the target article. For students, however, we feel we cannot assume such knowledge. The background information, then, is designed to serve an orienting function and to fill in any gaps we feel may have been left by the target article.

The really hard work for students and teachers comes in the third, **Talking points**, section of each chapter. The target articles have been selected not only because they are intrinsically interesting, but also because they give rise to important questions. The kinds of topics for discussion we have presented will, we feel, satisfy our aim in writing this book, namely the encouragement of critical thinking. We hope that the issues we address will give rise to lively discussion between teachers and students of psychology. What we haven't done is to provide any *answers* to the questions we pose, at least not in this book! The *Teacher's Guide*, which accompanies this book, does offer *some* potential solutions to the questions that are raised but even in the *Guide*, the solutions offered are neither prescriptive nor exhaustive. To labour the point, we want students to think critically about the discipline of psychology.

Finally, at the end of each chapter we have provided full references, as well as suggestions for further reading. The suggestions for further reading may offer some assistance in addressing the talking points.

This book is not intended to be read from cover to cover. We hope that each of the chapters is self-contained and that students and tutors will dip into the various chapters as and when the need arises. We have learnt much in the writing of this book. We hope that you learn more from using it.

Rob McIlveen
Martyn Long
Anthony Curtis

Acknowledgements

The authors and publishers would like to thank the following for their permission to reproduce copyright material:

The Guardian for articles 1, 3, 5, 6, and 7; *The Times* for article 2; Penguin Books Ltd for the table on p. 15; Jerome Burne for article 4; *The Daily Mail* for article 8; *The Independent on Sunday* for article 9; and finally, *The Observer* for article 10.

The authors would like to take this opportunity to thank the following for their encouragement, support and help in reviewing and commenting on the material contained in this book: Phil Banyard, Alun Bliss, Hugh Coolican, Simon Green, Richard Gross, Hedley Harnett, Mike Winton, and Alison Wadeley. Any errors that remain in the book are, of course, solely the responsibility of the authors. Thanks too to Tim Gregson-Williams and Louise Tooms at Hodder for their support throughout the production of this book. Without Tim's diplomatic skills, it might never have left the word processor.

1

LEFT BEHIND BY THE RIGHT MINDED

Left behind by the right minded

Liz Hodgkinson
© *The Guardian*

All my life I've laboured under a handicap. It means I cannot peel potatoes properly, cut out dress material or solve mathematical problems. Most tin-openers are beyond me and I cannot lay a table 'correctly'. I also have difficulty distinguishing right from left when giving directions.

On the other hand, my handicap means I can play a mean game of tennis, do mirror writing and am in touch with my imagination, intuition and feelings.

This handicap is one I share with Leonardo da Vinci, Charlie Chaplin, Paul McCartney, Esther Rantzen, Picasso, Prince Charles, Greta Garbo and Marilyn Monroe. Like these luminaries, I have been able to overcome it to a certain extent.

What is it? Simply, to be born left-handed in a predominately right-handed world. When you're left-handed, the world seems a funny place indeed. Cheque-book stubs are on the wrong side, and your natural inclination is to go from right to left when writing on a sheet of paper. Most domestic and everyday appliances, from irons to scissors, from cameras to car phones, are designed for right-handed people.

In many cases, left-handers cannot use the equipment at all. But instead of sympathy, left-handers are marked down for clumsiness and ineptitude.

When I was at infant school, I dreaded craft classes because I could not cut out paper or cardboard: the scissors had the cutting edge on the wrong side. When my cookery teacher saw me trying to prepare vegetables, she would just take the utensils out of my hand, 'as it all looked so dangerous'.

For me, as for many schoolchildren in the fifties, left-handedness was not taken into account. The idea persisted that we were deliberately sabotaging and disrupting attempts to teach us handicrafts or cookery. In those days, of course, there was no such thing as a pair of left-handed scissors.

But even then, I was lucky. If I'd been born a few years earlier I might have been forced to write with my right hand, like King George VI. I might then have developed a stammer and other emotional problems.

But according to the book *Living Left Handed*, by left-hander Diane Paul, things have hardly improved. Although between 10 and 15 per cent of the population are left-handed, and are allowed to stay that way, it is difficult to obtain the appropriate utensils.

Since biblical times, left-handers have received a very bad press. Good people sit on the right hand of God. The 'bend sinister' in heraldry is (or was) reserved for bastard heirs. The Latin word for left is *sinistra*, the French word is *gauche* – both carry unattractive connotations

To affirm something we say 'right', not 'left'. If something is correct, it is 'right', not 'left'. An indispensible assistant is a 'right-hand man'. A compliment with a nasty sting is considered 'left-handed'.

In India, where children are still made to use their right hands, it is thought shocking bad manners to pick up food or cutlery with the left hand. This hand, in Eastern culture, is reserved for cleaning up after a visit to the lavatory.

The question is, why should the right-hand predominate? Despite research over the past 20 years, nobody really knows. Theories abound: that left-handedness is caused by a mild degree of brain damage at birth, by a difficult delivery, or by too much of the male hormone testosterone circulating prenatally.

According to this theory, propounded by the late Norman Geschwind, Professor of Neurology at Harvard Medical School, 10 times more left-handers than right show a strong inclination towards dyslexia and stammering. Professor Geschwind claimed that the connection between all three handicaps was too much pre-birth testosterone, which slows down the brain's development and gives rise to cells in the brain that should not be there.

His research indicated there is a high incidence of dyslexia, autism, epilepsy, speech problems, hyperactivity and stammering among left-handers. More boys than girls, he found, were left-handed, and there was also a high incidence among identical twins.

Left-handedness appears to be an aberration, rather than the norm. Research carried out by Dr Peter Hepper, of Queen's University Belfast, found only 5.4 per cent of foetuses showed a preference for the left thumb when thumb-sucking in the womb.

'Left-handedness,' says Diane Paul, 'has proved the greatest enigma to science of all time – and it still hasn't been completely solved.'

But there are compensations. Although largely useless around mechanical equipment, research shows left-handers are gifted, original, creative – and have more immediate access to the right hemisphere of the brain, which governs creativity and intuition.

Since the fifties left-handed tennis champions have included Ann Jones, Martina Navratilova, John McEnroe, Jimmy Connors, Roscoe Tanner, Rod Laver, Tony Roche and Guillermo Vilas.

Perhaps left-handers should leave the mundane jobs to right-handed people, while they get on with playing tennis and indulging their imaginations and creative brilliance.

Background

Psychologists have long been interested in the concept of 'handedness' or 'hand preference' and a number of ways of assessing it have been devised. One of the most well known is the Edinburgh Handedness Inventory (Oldfield, 1971) which assesses skills that can only be performed by one hand at a time, such as writing, drawing and throwing. Studies have shown that on tasks which allow freedom of hand choice, about 90 per cent of people show a consistent preference for the right hand and about 7 to 8 per cent for the left hand. The remaining 2 to 3 per cent can be described as 'mixed-handed' since their hand preference varies according to the task or action concerned (even though one hand is usually preferred for any particular action: Annett, 1992). Contrary to popular belief, very few people are ambidextrous, that is, can use both hands equally well for the same task (Springer & Deutsch, 1989).

In most people there is a contralateral relationship between hand control and the cerebral hemispheres. Most of the nerves sensing and controlling the hands, cross over in the base of the brain. The right hand is usually controlled by the left half of the brain and vice versa. The relationship between handedness and cerebral organisation has been the subject of much research, and suggests that hand preference is linked to the specialisation of the cerebral hemispheres. The study of handedness is thus important since it is an external sign of an underlying lateral specialisation of the brain. A close investigation of handedness can provide us with insights into the basic organisation and functioning of the brain.

In the vast majority (i.e 95 per cent) of right-handers (or 'dextrals') the left half of the brain has the major involvement in language via cortical areas (such as Broca's area in the frontal lobe and Wernicke's area in the temporal lobe) which are not present in the other hemisphere. For right-handers, the left hemisphere is usually specialised for the logical and sequential processing of words and grammar and for assembling speech. In the majority of right-handers, the right hemisphere plays only a restricted role in language and is better at perceiving spatial relationships and recognising shapes. For some researchers (e.g. Ornstein, 1977) hand preference is associated with the 'linguistic hemisphere' because the use and control of the hands is essentially sequential. As Annett (1992) has remarked, however, the question of whether the connection between the left hemisphere's role in language and right-handedness is causal or accidental has no generally accepted answer at present.

Although we might expect the brain organisation of left-handers (or 'sinistrals') to be the mirror image of that for right-handers, the situation is actually much more complex; it is made even more complex by the fact that different techniques to assess both linguistic competence of the hemispheres and handedness yield slightly different data! It is true that for about 15 per cent of left-handers the right hemisphere is dominant for language. However, the left hemisphere has the major involvement in language for about 70 per cent of left-handers (Milner, 1974; Springer & Deutsch, 1989). In the remaining 15 per cent of left-handers, language is bilaterally represented, indicating more of a functional hemispheric symmetry rather than the more usual asymmetry (Green, 1991).

Sandra Wittelson (e.g. Wittelson, 1985) has undertaken much research looking at anatomical differences in the brains of right and left-handers. In one study, the handedness of 42 terminally ill cancer patients was assessed. Wittelson later conducted post-mortem analyses on the brains of the deceased. One structure Wittleson investigated was the corpus callosum, a large bundle of nerve fibres which joins the two cerebral hemispheres together. The corpus callosum connects regions of the cerebral hemispheres which are physically opposite each other, and functionally complementary, and allows the specialisations of the two hemispheres to be coordinated.

In those patients who were either consistently or at least partially left-handed, the corpus callosum was on average 11 per cent larger. Since the corpus callosum consists of around 200 million nerve fibres in right-handed people, Wittelson's data suggested that complete or partial left-handers have around 25 million more nerve fibres connecting the two hemispheres. This greater neuronal link between the hemispheres might explain the fact that cognitive functions like language tend to be more lateralised for right than left-handers.

Like humans, the brains of non-human animals show some specialisations and these become more similar to human differences the closer the animal is phylogenetically to humans (Bradshaw, 1991). However, although animals often show a strong paw, claw or even fin preference, left or right are almost equally as likely to be favoured, and are easily influenced by environmental variables such as training and object position (Trevarthen, 1978). The only exception to this appears to be the parrot which is apparently left-clawed (Rogers, 1980), though why this is the case is not known.

In proto-humans, fossil baboon skulls which had been fractured with bone or wooden clubs by Austalopithecines, an early relative of humans, indicate predominantly right-handedness (Hardyk & Petrinovich, 1977). It has been suggested that handedness in humans first appeared in the lower stone age when toolmaking became common. Some of the tools discovered from that period seem to have been made by right-handers for right-handed use (Flowers, 1987). People depicted in ancient Egyptian tomb paintings were also predominantly right-handed (Hassett & White, 1989).

It has been proposed that there is an inherited (genetic) bias towards right-handedness and left-hemisphere language specialisation (e.g Annett, 1964). Some studies (e.g. Galaburda, 1984) have shown that the number of ridges on the fingerprints of foetuses during the third and fourth months of gestation is larger in the right hand than the left, a preponderance which persists throughout foetal life and after birth

(Sagan, 1978). Left-handedness also appears to run in families. Rife (1940) reported that when both parents are left-handed, about 45 per cent of their children are left-handed. If only one parent is left-handed the figure is 30 per cent, and if neither parent is left-handed the figure is only 8 per cent. Using sophisticated scanning devices, other researchers (e.g. Habib, 1989) have revealed evidence of very early physical differences in the brains of left-handers.

On the basis of these findings it has been suggested that heritability may be an important factor in left-handedness, possibly as a gene which prevents the development of 'normal dextrality' (Annett, 1985). Several other genetic models have been proposed (e.g. Levy & Nagylaki, 1972) although the evidence for a genetic basis to handedness is far from conclusive. For example, even in monozygotic twins (who share the same genes) one quarter have opposite handedness (Springer & Deutsch, 1989).

Hand preference has also been investigated in connection with a number of cerebral functions other than language. For example, the majority of right-handers show a right-ear advantage when listening to speech and a left-ear advantage for listening to music. Emotional expression and perception is specialised in the right hemisphere for right-handers. Expressions on the left side of the face (which is right hemisphere controlled) therefore show more of right-hander's emotional state (Rubin & Rubin, 1980). Large scale research on handedness is a relatively recent phenomenon and researchers are only just beginning to reach an understanding of it.

Talking points

1 Several studies (e.g. Annett, 1985) have suggested that left-handers appear with greater frequency than would be expected among top sportsmen and women. The article identifies a large number of left-handed tennis players of both sexes who have been very successful in their careers. These include Laver, Vilas, McEnroe, Jones, Tanner and Navratilova. Goran Ivanisevic is perhaps the most successful of the recent left-handed players. In baseball, the legendary 'Babe' Ruth was bullied into right-handedness in the orphanage where he grew up, but hit all of his home runs left-handed. In boxing, the left-handed Marvin Hagler had an enviable record, whilst cricket numbers Sobers, Lloyd, Border and Gower among its most successful left-handed performers.

It has been proposed that left-handers have superior spatio-motor skills as compared with right-handers and that this innate superiority accounts for their over-representation as top performers in sports. Such a proposal may be appealing for left-handers, but what alternative explanations do you think might account for left-handers' success in certain sporting activities?

2 The author of the article bemoans her fate of being 'born left-handed in a predominantly right-handed world'. As she notes, cheque-book stubs are on the 'wrong' side, and most domestic appliances are designed for right-handed people. Scissors with the cutting edge on the 'wrong' side made the author dread her craft classes and in cookery her attempts to prepare vegetables were considered 'dangerous' by her cookery teacher. What other objects and utensils do you think left-handers would find difficult to use? How would you explain the increased accident rate that has been claimed (e.g. Bracha, Seitz, Otemaa & Glick, 1987) for left-handers?

3 According to the article 'left-handedness ... has proved the greatest enigma to science of all time – and it still hasn't been completely solved'. As indicated in both the article and the **Background** there have been several attempts to account for left-handedness. These range from theories proposing that left-handedness is produced by social pressure or early experiences to those based on the role of genetic factors. One recent and provocative theory has been advanced by Norman Geschwind (e.g. 1983, 1984).

Geschwind and his colleagues conducted several surveys of over 2 000 people. As well as confirming the observation that left-handers seem to be more likely to suffer from dyslexia and other learning difficulties, Geschwind discovered that left-handers were three times as likely to suffer from immune disorders as right-handers, and their relatives were twice as likely to have these disorders as the rest of the population. In what ways do you think biological factors might be causally related to handedness? The material presented in both the article and the **Background** is a useful starting point.

4 The article notes that 'since biblical times, left-handers have received a very bad press' as compared with right-handers. 'Sinistra' (also meaning sinister) is the Latin word and 'gauche' (also meaning clumsiness) the French word for left. As the article suggests, both carry unfavourable connotations. In what other ways, apart from those mentioned in the article, could left-handedness be said to have received 'a very bad press'?

5 The lot of the left-hander several decades ago was certainly not a happy one. The author of the article suggests that, in Britain, left-handed children were once perceived as attempting to sabotage and disrupt attempts to be taught handicrafts or cookery. Left-handedness was also seen as an aberration to be 'corrected', if possible, even if this meant forcing the child to write with the right hand by tying down the preferred left hand. Most present day Western societies are now relatively tolerant of left-handedness. If you had a child who did not seem to have developed a particular hand dominance when s/he started school at the age of five (an age when the hand preference of most children is fairly well established) would you want your child to be encouraged to use a particular hand for writing? If not, why not?

6 Being left-handed is not all negative! As noted earlier, in some sports it appears to confer an advantage at least when the competition is against a right-hander. As the article suggests Picasso, da Vinci, Monroe, Chaplin, McCartney and Garbo were all able to 'overcome' their left-handedness and achieve eminence in the field of art and entertainment. To this list can be added (amongst others) the abstract artist Paul Klee, the comedian Harpo Marx, and the rock guitarist Jimi Hendrix.

Do you think that the more complex pattern of brain organisation found in left-handers could have anything to do with the author of the article's claim that they are 'gifted, original [and] creative'? How would you explain the seemingly well-established over-representation of left-handers in mathematics (e.g. Benbow & Stanley, 1983)? What alternative explanations for this over-representation do you think could be advanced?

7 As noted in the **Background**, the left hemisphere is, for the majority of people, usually dominant in language and controls the (usually) dominant right hand. If this is inherited, it must have some evolutionary value, that is, right-handers must have been more likely in the past to survive and reproduce. What advantages do you think right-handedness could have conferred?

When both parents are left-handed there is a 50 per cent chance that an offspring will also be left-handed (Annett, 1964). If right-handedness is the inherited norm which *does* confer certain advantages, then a deviation from this should be a disadvantage and, over time, be selected out! Evidently, then, left-handedness too must confer some advantages or it would have disappeared over time. What possible advantages could left-handedness have conferred? In evolutionary terms, do you think it is more likely that the development of language determined handedness or that the development of handedness determined the laterality of language?

8 Various writers (e.g. Bogen, 1975) have hypothesised that the educational process is excessively dominated by sequential skills which involve structured language or arithmetic skills. These are typical right-handed, left-brain, abilities and Bogen proposes that an emphasis on these might detract from more holistic, right-hemisphere abilities. What educational activities do you think could be used to involve more of the holistic processing hemisphere and how could these be integrated into the curriculum? What possible advantages might be derived from developing such abilities?

Recently, Caine and Caine (1990) have advocated integrating left-analytic and right-spatial features. This holistic (non-lateralised) style of learning should involve 'orchestrated immersion', 'relaxed alertness' and 'active processing'. How could you enhance personal involvement, relevance, and the linking together of separate areas in your study of psychology? Has the process of using this book helped you achieve this?

9 Estimates of left-handedness have often varied quite dramatically. The article suggests a figure of 10–15 per cent of the population whilst in the **Background** the figure suggested was about 7–8 per cent! Flowers (1987) reports that the proportion has been variously reported as being 4–36 per cent. One way to assess your own handedness is to use one of the several handedness inventories. Annett's (1970) inventory asks which hand is habitually used for 12 activities (possible responses being 'right', 'left' or 'either'). The inventory and a person's classification on the basis of their responses can be found in Annett (1992).

As noted in the **Background**, hand preference has been investigated in connection with a number of cerebral functions other than language. Based on your handedness, is your preference consistent with research findings?

References and further reading

Those references which are particularly worthy of further concern are indicated thus: *, together with a brief description of their area of concern.

Annett, M. (1964) 'A model of the inheritance of handedness and cerebral dominance', *Nature*, 204, pp. 59–60.

Annett, M. (1970) 'A classification of hand preference by association analysis', *British Journal of Psychology*, 61, pp. 641–52.

*Annett, M. (1985) *Left, Right, Hand and Brain: The Right Shift Theory*, London: Lawrence Earlbaum Associates. *This is Annett's most complete description of her theory of the heritability of cerebral specialisation and handedness.*

Annett, M. (1992) 'Hand preference and hand skill', **in** R. McIlveen, L. Higgins, A. Wadeley & P. Humphreys, (Eds.) *The BPS Manual of Psychology Practicals*, Leicester: BPS Books.

Benbow, C.P. & Stanley, J.C. (1983) 'Sex differences in mathematical reasoning ability', *Science*, 222, pp. 1029–31.

Bogen, J. (1975) 'Some educational aspects of hemispheric specialisation', *UCLA Educator*, 17, pp. 24-32.

Bracha, H., Seitz, D., Otemaa, J. & Glick, S. (1987) 'Rotational movement (circling) in normal humans: sex differences and relationship to hand, foot and eye preference', *Brain Research*, 41, pp. 231–5.

*Bradshaw, J. (1991) 'Animal asymmetry and human heredity: dextrality, tool use and language in evolution – 10 years after Walker (1980)', *British Journal of Psychology*, 82, pp. 39–59. *An excellent and accessible review of the evolutionary basis of handedness related to the early development of language.*

Caine, R. & Caine, G. (1990) 'Understanding a brain-based approach to learning and teaching', *Educational Leadership*, 48, pp. 66–70.

Flowers, K.A.F. (1987) 'Handedness', **in** R.L. Gregory (Ed.) *The Oxford Companion to the Mind*. Oxford: Oxford University Press.

Galaburda, A. (1984) 'Anatomical asymmetries in the human brain', **in** N. Geschwind & A. Galaburda (Eds.), *Biological Foundations of Cerebral Dominance*, Cambridge, MA: Harvard University Press.

*Geschwind, N. (1983) 'Biological associations of left-handedness', *Annals of Dyslexia*, 33, pp. 29–40. *This article describes Geshwind's views on the differential susceptibilities of right and left-handers to various disorders.*

Geschwind, N. (1984) 'The biology of cerebral dominance: Implications for cognition', *Cognition*, 17, pp. 193–208.

Green, S. (1991) 'Physiological Studies II', **in** J. Radford & E. Govier (Eds.) *A Textbook of Psychology* (2nd ed.) London: Routledge.

Habib, M. (1989) 'Anatomical asymmetries of the human cerebral cortex', *International Journal of Neuroscience*, 47, pp. 67–79.

*Hardyk, C. & Petrinovich, L.F. (1977) 'Left-handedness', *Psychological Bulletin*, 84, pp. 385–404. *Although a little dated now, this is an interesting review of research in the area.*

Hassett, J. & White, K.M. (1989) *Psychology in Perspective*, London: Harper & Row.

Levy, J. & Nagylaki, T. (1972) 'A model for the genetics of handedness', *Genetics*, 72, pp. 117–28.

Milner, B. (1974) 'Hemispheric specialisation: scope and limits', **in** F. Schmitt & F. Warden (Eds.) *The Neurosciences: Third Study Program*, Cambridge, MA: MIT Press.

Oldfield, R. (1971) 'The assessment and analysis of handedness: The Edinburgh Inventory', *Neuropsychologica*, 9, pp. 97–114.

Ornstein, R. (1977) *The Psychology of Consciousness*, Chicago: Harcourt, Brace, Jovanovich.

Rife, D.C. (1940) 'Handedness, with special reference to twins', *Genetics*, 25, pp. 178–86.

Rogers, L. (1980) 'Lateralisation in the avian brain', *Bird Behaviour*, 2, pp. 1–12.

Rubin, D. & Rubin, T. (1980) 'Differences in asymmetry of facial expression between right and left-handed children', *Neuropsychologica*, 18, pp. 373–77.

Sagan, C. (1978) *The Dragons of Eden*, London: Hodder & Stoughton.

*Springer, S.P. & Deutsch, G. (1989) *Left Brain, Right Brain*, New York: W.H. Freeman. *Springer and Deutsch provide a very readable introduction to the study of handedness.*

Trevarthen, C. (1978) 'Manipulative strategies of baboons and origins of cerebral asymmetry', **in** M. Kinsbourne (Ed.) *Asymmetrical Function of the Brain*, Cambridge, Cambridge University Press.

Wittelson, S.F. (1985) 'The brain connection: the corpus collosum is larger in left-handers', *Science*, 229, pp. 665–8.

2

WHO IS THE REAL ME?

Who is the real me?

© Simon Wessely
The Times
30/12/93

Oscar Wilde wrote: 'I am certain that I have three separate or distinct souls.' Would he nowadays have been diagnosed as suffering from multiple personality disorder?

The problem of individuals with a single body, but who behave as if they are two or more personalities, has a long history. Perhaps the most famous example was Eve White, a shy withdrawn girl being treated for unexplained headaches, who during psychotherapy suddenly would become another person, Eve Black, who was bright, flirtatious and over-confident.

A third personality, Jane, made her appearance after more psychotherapy. Thigpen and Cleckley, a psychologist and a psychiatrist, revealed her story in the book *The Three Faces of Eve*. Eve was not the first, but was certainly the best known, case of multiple personality disorder (MPD).

Thirty years later, Thigpen and Cleckley returned to the subject of MPD. In a 1984 paper they discussed the epidemic of MPD that had swept the United States since the publication of their book. One might have expected them to be pleased with this recognition, but they were not.

Thigpen and Cleckley revealed that since the publication of *The Three Faces of Eve* they had been referred many thousands of people who strenuously sought to be diagnosed as having MPD. In order to see the doctors, many of the patients used various voices on the telephone, or wrote letters to them in different handwriting. However, Thigpen and Cleckley diagnosed only one further case of MPD.

The authors noted that many of these patients went from therapist to therapist until they found some doctor who would accept the label of MPD. Thigpen and Cleckley noted with regret that a competition seemed to have developed among some doctors to see who could diagnose the most cases. They might also have added 'and whose cases could have the most personalities'.

A recent survey showed that the average MPD patient in the US now has eight separate personalities. A recent book was written by one sufferer who had 95 personalities, known as the 'Troops', most of whom had contributed to the text.

MPD has become an epidemic in America, with its own journal. Frequent conferences are held on the topic, during which, as one observer put it, 'therapists show videos of their patients producing their latest cute tricks'.

Some have suggested that MPD is a form of psychosis, others that it is a modern variation of spirit possession. Most favour either psychological or social explanations. One is reminiscent of the Jekyll and Hyde story. MPD may provide a way in which subjects can escape responsibility for those aspects of their personality they find unacceptable.

Another survey noted that it was common among cases to attribute antisocial acts that they had performed to their other selves as a way of avoiding blame. In America, MPD has been used as a successful defence in rape and other serious crimes.

The most notorious example was the case of Kenneth Bianchi, known as the 'Hillside Strangler', responsible for a series of horrific murders of young women in Los Angeles. Bianchi's defence was one of multiple personality.

Psychiatrists experienced in MPD were convinced by his performance, until a more sceptical expert proved Bianchi to be faking. Far from being psychologically naïve, as he claimed, he had in fact previously impersonated a psychologist, and had a considerable knowledge of psychological methods and jargon. He originally claimed to be two people, but when casually told by the psychiatrist that most cases of MPD had three personalities, promptly produced a third on cue.

One of the defence psychiatrists later admitted that it had never occurred to him that subjects, even when facing the death penalty, might lie.

Usually people who claim to have MPD have long histories of a variety of psychiatric disorders. Most have been in therapy for some years. Many report traumatic childhoods, with stories of neglect, deprivation and abuse.

Proponents of MPD argue that the experience of abuse at an early age has led to the child developing psychological coping mechanisms including denial of what is happening, ignoring its meaning, or retreating into a fantasy life. This leads to a psychological defence known as dissociation, in which different aspects of personality and memory can, at times, be repressed.

All of us act in different ways at different times. To be inconsistent is normal, even if inconvenient for ourselves and others. All of us have experienced our 'minds going blank', or have forgotten things we would rather not remember. In a recent survey, 65 per cent of children had imaginary play-mates.

Critics of MPD argue that in disturbed individuals, these traits become amplified in a manner that is only quantitatively, and not qualitatively, different from normal.

In this country the diagnosis is almost unknown. Is this simply because we don't look for it? Perhaps, but more likely it is because British psychiatrists do not act in a way that will lead to the creation of multiple personalities in our patients. We fail to respond to the cues that might lead a distressed, suggestible patient, trying to come to terms with an awful past, to develop symptoms of MPD.

Some of our American colleagues, in a similar situation, behave differently. Some therapists now use hypnosis to uncover the alternative personality, or in other ways actively encourage the patient to dissociate and produce more and more alternative personalities.

In America, a frequent technique is to address the different personalities as if they are different people – giving each an age, name, sex, profession and complete biography.

This has led to the farcical situation reported in a Wisconsin court in which a witness was sworn in three times, once for each of her personalities. Another 40 did not give evidence, including one which 'evolved from a small animal which lives beneath the table and growls when frightened'.

Dr Tom Fahy, of the Institute of Psychiatry, a critic of MPD, has described cases in which the number of alternate personalities is proportional to the number of years in therapy. Patients who develop MPD may be subjects who have learnt to cope with previous trauma by dissociation, but now have found a therapist who will collude in this new, dramatic piece of theatre. The therapist is thus acting as the midwife for the new personalities.

We must beware in this country of an uncritical acceptance of the existence of MPD. Digby Tantam, Professor of Psychotherapy at Warwick University, says that before a new psychiatric diagnosis is accepted, certain safeguards are needed.

First, that the diagnosis itself does not create new symptoms. Second, that the diagnosis does not increase disability. Third, that it does not lead to dependency on the therapist.

At the moment, MPD fails all three tests. Professor Tantam concluded that he found the business of MPD embarrassing. As long as British psychiatrists remain embarrassed, and not fascinated, by this phenomenon, multiple personality disorder may remain restricted to fiction and American court rooms.

Background

Of all the mental disorders recognised by psychiatric classificatory systems, perhaps the most bizarre and least well understood is multiple personality disorder (MPD). In MPD, a single individual is dominated by two or more distinct, integrated and well-developed personalities or personal states at different points in time. MPD is classified as a dissociative disorder, that is, a disorder characterised by sudden, temporary and dramatic changes in memory, identity and other complex psychological functions.

In its most basic form MPD is termed 'alternating personality': two personalities alternate, each unaware of the thoughts and behaviours of the other. As DSM-3-R notes, in the classic cases, the personalities and personal states each have unique memories, behaviour patterns and social relationships. In more complex forms of the disorder, personalities 'eavesdrop' on their rivals when one personality is 'dominant' and controlling the person's behaviour. The so-called 'subordinate' personalities are thus fully aware of the thoughts and the behaviours of the dominant personality, and are said to be 'coconscious' with the dominant personality (Prince, 1905). Yet whilst the subordinate personalities are aware of the dominant personality, the latter is often unaware of the former. Coconscious personalities are able to express their awareness through 'automatic writing' (in which a person writes a message without awareness or conscious control) or some other indirect way.

Perhaps because of its dramatic nature, cases of MPD are particularly well documented. Some of the most famous cases can be found in Thigpen and Cleckley (1954, 1957), Schreiber (1973), Osgood, Luria, Jeans and Smith (1976), Sizemore and Pitillo (1977), Keyes (1982) and Casey (1993). In some instances the sub-personality or personalities are so different from the core personality that they can be described as 'polar opposites'. Thus, if one personality is 'conformist' and 'nice', the other will be 'rebellious' and 'nasty'. A case-study reported by Lipton (1943), which involved two personalities, 'Maud K.' and 'Sara', provides a good illustration of this:

> In general demeanour, Maud was quite different from Sara. She walked with a swinging, bouncing gait contrasted to Sara's sedate one. While Sara was depressed, Maud was ebullient and happy ... Maud used a lot of rouge and lipstick, painted her fingernails and toenails deep red, and put a red ribbon in her hair. She liked red and was quickly attracted by anything of that colour. Sara's favourite colour was blue. Sara was a mature, intelligent individual. Her IQ [was] 128 (Maud's IQ was 43) ... Sara did not smoke and was very awkward when she attempted it. Maud had a compulsion to smoke ... Maud had no conscience, no sense of right and wrong. She saw no reason for not always doing as she pleased. She felt no guilt over her incestuous and promiscuous sexual relationships. Sara on the other hand had marked guilt feelings over her previous immoral behaviour.

It has been suggested (e.g. Greaves, 1980) that MPD begins following a serious emotional or other traumatic event during childhood, and usually occurs around the age of four to six. According to Frischholz (1985), a child copes with a painful problem by creating another personality to bear the brunt of the difficulty. One 'identifiable stressor precipitant' is sexual abuse. Coons, Milstein and Marley (1982) describe the case of 'Lucy' a 23-year-old woman who was sexually abused by an alcoholic father at the age of five. Lucy was raped at the age of 21, and began having frequent periods of amnesia and headaches (Lucy had in fact experienced amnesia from the age of five). Lucy had at least three other personalities:

> Linda, the personality who originated at age five was confident, aggressive, and normally good humoured, but would fly into a rage at the slightest provocation. Sally, a personality formed to cope with the rape experience, was reclusive, distrustful and nearly mute. Sam, a male secondary personality, served as a rescuer personality when Sally made one of her many suicide attempts.

As suggested above, transitions from one personality to another are often triggered by traumatic or stressful events, and periods of severe headache followed by unexplained amnesia are typically taken as being suggestive of MPD. Personality alteration may vary from minutes to a period of years, although the former is more common. In at least some cases, personality alteration is marked by changes in body posture and tone of voice, and there is some evidence that changes in physiological and neurological activity may accompany personality alteration (Goleman, 1985).

Physiological and neurological changes were documented in a study reported by Ludwig, Brandsma, Wilbur, Benfeldt and Jameson (1972). Jonah, a 27-year-old man, was admitted to hospital complaining of severe headaches and lapses of memory. During his stay, hospital attendants noticed changes in Jonah's personality whenever these episodes occurred. In addition to the primary personality of Jonah who was a shy, polite and highly conventional individual, three distinct personalities were identified by Ludwig and his associates.

The first, 'Sammy', remembered emerging at the age of six when Jonah's mother stabbed his stepfather and Sammy persuaded the parents never to fight again in front of the children. Sammy was aware of the other personalities and could coexist in consciousness with Jonah or set Jonah aside and take over. Sammy emerged every time Jonah was in trouble or needed legal advice. Sammy, the intellectual and rational personality, was designated 'the lawyer' (in contrast to Jonah's designation as 'the square').

The second personality, 'King Young' emerged when Jonah was six or seven, and was only indirectly aware of the other personalities. Jonah's mother had occasionally dressed him in girl's clothes and Jonah had become confused about his sexual identity. Glib, and very much a ladies man, King Young emerged whenever Jonah encountered difficulties with women. He was designated 'the lover'. 'Usoffa Abdulla', designated 'the warrior', was the third personality. He emerged when Jonah was 10 and a gang of boys beat him up without provocation. When Jonah lost consciousness, Usoffa took over and was so violent that he nearly killed several of the boys. Aware of Jonah, but only indirectly aware of the others, Usoffa's role was to protect and watch over Jonah. Capable of ignoring pain, Usoffa appeared at the first sign of physical danger to Jonah and left after the problem had been (usually violently) resolved.

Ludwig and his colleagues asked each of the four personalities to supply words of personal emotional significance. For each personality two of these words were then selected and interspersed with twelve neutral words, giving a total of twenty words. Each personality was then presented with the twenty words and his galvanic skin response was measured. The results showed that whilst Jonah responded to the emotional words of the other personalities, they responded only to their own words and demonstrated little response to the words supplied by other personalities. Each personality was also assessed by means of an electroencephalogram (EEG). Some of the measures obtained are shown below:

Measure	Jonah	Sammy	King Young	Usoffa
Alpha wave Freq. (Cps)	10.5	9.5	9.5	10.5
Alpha wave Amp. (mVolts)	20.0	20.0	30.0	15.0
% time Alpha wave	53.0	20.0	52.0	41.0
% time Delta wave	31.0	75.0	18.0	45.0

Source: R.F. Schreiber (1973) *Sybil*, Penguin.

In addition to the differences shown by EEG, other interesting findings were obtained. For example, unlike the other personalities, Usoffa Abdulla ('the warrior') had a markedly reduced sense of pain. He displayed a hysterical conversion reaction (hypalgesia) which meant that portions of his body were immune to pain (Sue, Sue & Sue, 1990).

Talking points

1 Although several attempts have been made to validate the existence of MPD, the author of the article is clearly sceptical, a scepticism shared by many others. For example, Carlson (1987) has suggested that at least some cases of MPD 'are simulations, not actual mental disorders'. Berman (1975) and Spanos, Weekes and Bertrand (1985) have shown that MPD can be induced experimentally using hypnosis. Sceptics contend that this supports the view that many apparent cases of MPD are in fact faked.

Arguing from a social learning perspective, Thigpen and Cleckley (1984) propose that features of MPD can be role-played through observational learning. Spanos, et al. (1985) argue that the portrayal of MPD in films, on television, and in books has made the disorder well known, and provided 'detailed examples of the symptoms and course of multiple personality'. In what circumstances do you think a person might be motivated to role-play the characteristics of MPD for personal gain? What sort of mental disorder could a person motivated to role-play MPD actually be experiencing?

2 As Sue, Sue and Sue (1990) have commented, the diagnosis of all dissociative disorders is not straightforward because of the reliance on the individual's self-reports. Since, as the article suggests, some psychiatrists might not even contemplate the possibility that an individual is lying, differentiating between the fraudulent and the genuine can be difficult. With respect to amnesia, for example, Schacter (1986) has shown that even expert judges find it difficult to distinguish between simulated amnesia and the genuine inability to recall.

The possibility that a person is feigning or faking a disorder can, however, be investigated in a number of ways. For example, Bradford and Smith (1979) used sodium amytal (the so-called 'truth drug') to test the claims of several accused murderers that they were suffering from amnesia when the act was committed. Using information presented in the article and the **Background**, how would you attempt to show that person apparently experiencing MPD was actually faking?

3 In connection with the above, Carson, Butcher and Coleman (1988) have proposed that because MPD can be induced experimentally, it might be the case that the disorder 'is an artificial creation produced inadvertently by suggestions of the therapist'. Put another way, MPD occurs when a potential 'sufferer' encounters a therapist who either believes in, or is interested in, the disorder. Quoting Thigpen and Cleckley, authors of *The Three Faces of Eve* which describes arguably the most famous of all MPD cases, the article suggests that 'a competition [seems] to have developed among some doctors to see who could diagnose the most cases ... and whose cases could have the most personalities'.

In support of this view, Bootzin and Acocella (1984) have argued that since most cases of MPD 'have turned up in the United States, where public interest in this disorder seems greatest', some cases 'may have been unwittingly encouraged by therapists eager for publicity'. As the article suggests, by finding 'therapist who will collude in this new dramatic piece of theatre ... the therapist [acts] as the midwife for the new personalities'. How could you test Carson and his colleagues' proposal that MPD is an artificial creation produced inadvertently by suggestions of the therapist? What do you think Carson and his colleagues mean when they suggest that a potential MPD's behaviour may involve 'elements of "performance" whose deliberateness is less consciously contrived than it is an absorption in the "role" '?

4 The article suggests that 'in America, a frequent technique is to address different personalities as if they are different people – giving each an age, name, sex, profession and complete biography.' The article briefly describes a court case in Wisconsin, USA in which a Mark Peterson was tried for the rape of a Korean-born woman identified in court as 'Sarah'. The trial attracted much publicity because Sarah was alleged to possess an incredible 46 personalities, including 'Sam' the creature that 'evolved from a small animal which lives beneath tables and growls when frightened'.

In essence, the prosecution claimed that Peterson knew Sarah was suffering from MPD and used this knowledge to have intercourse with one 'willing' personality. Under a Wisconsin state law it is illegal for a person to have sex with someone who is unable to assess his or her own conduct. After six hours deliberation the jury decided Peterson did know that Sarah was unable to assess her own conduct and thus was guilty as charged. What sorts of evidence would you feel were necessary before Peterson could be found guilty or innocent? During the case, a leading member of the Chicago Bar Association said 'There are many women who wake up the next morning and say "I wish I hadn't done it". They are now asking courts to prosecute the man involved because the woman said "I wasn't my real self when I said yes". This has got to go to appeal'. Do you agree?

5 According to Coons and Bradley (1985) and Kluft (1987), MPD is much more prevalent in females, who, as noted elsewhere, often report having experienced a serious or traumatic event during childhood. Greaves (1980) and Fagan and McMahon (1984) have reported that physical and/or sexual abuse are the most commonly documented events. Although the causal connection between early childhood experiences and subsequent MPD has not been confirmed, some psychiatrists and psychologists believe it to exist.

As the article suggests, 'the experience of abuse at an early age [leads, according to its proponents] to a child developing psychological coping mechanisms including denial of what is happening, ignoring its meaning or retreating into a fantasy life'. This leads to 'a psychological defence known as dissociation, in which different parts of the personality can, at times, be repressed'. What psychological perspective is the author of the article describing and how could MPD be accounted for within it? Could any other perspectives also be used to explain the origins of MPD?

6 If MPD is a real disorder, then it is clearly incumbent upon the caring professions to attempt to treat it. Unfortunately because MPD (if it exists) is not well understood, it has proved difficult to treat. One approach has been to combine hypnosis and psychotherapy. Initially, hypnosis is used to make the different personalities known to the core personality who thus becomes aware of their existence. Then, each personality is asked to recall the traumatic event(s) which led to its emergence, and to relive the associated emotions in order to deal with them in a supportive situation. Events and memories from the different personalities are then pieced together in order to integrate them into one. Psychotherapy without hypnosis may then follow, helping the individual adjust to the new self. What other therapeutic approaches do you think could be used to treat MPD and what techniques would be involved in these approaches?

References and further reading

Those references which are particularly worthy of further reading are indicated thus: *, together with a brief description of their area of concern.

Berman, E. (1975) 'Tested and documented split personality: Veronica and Nelly', *Psychology Today*, August, pp. 78–81.

Bootzin, R.R. & Acocella, J.R. (1984) *Abnormal Psychology: Current Perspectives*, New York: Random House.

Bradford, J.W. & Smith, S.M. (1979) 'Amnesia and homicide: The Padula case and a study of thirty cases', *Bulletin of the American Academy of Psychiatry and Law*, 7, pp. 219–31.

Carlson, N.R. (1987) *Discovering Psychology*, London: Allyn & Bacon.

Carson, R.C., Butcher, J.N. & Coleman, J.C. (1988) *Abnormal Psychology and Everyday Life*, London: Scott, Foresman & Company.

Casey, J. (1993) *The Flock*, London: Abacus.

Coons, P.M. & Bradley, K. (1985) 'Group psychotherapy with multiple personality patients', *Journal of Nervous and Mental Diseases*, 173, pp. 515–21.

Coons, P.M., Milstein, V. & Marley, C. (1982) 'EEG studies of two multiple personalities and a control', *Archives of General Psychiatry*, 39, p. 823–5.

Fagan, J. & McMahon, P.P. (1984) 'Incipient multiple personality in children: four cases', *Journal of Nervous and Mental Disease*, 172, pp. 26–36.

Frischholz, E.J. (1985) 'The relationship among dissociation, hypnosis and child abuse in the development of multiple personality disorder', **in** Kluft, R. (Ed.) *Childhood Antecedents of Multiple Personality*, Washington, D.C.: American Psychiatric Association Press.

Goleman, D. (1985) 'New focus on multiple personality', *The New York Times*, May 21, C1 & C6.

Greaves, G.B. (1980) 'Multiple personality: 165 years after Mary Reynolds', *Journal of Nervous and Mental Disease*, 168, pp. 577–96.

*Keyes, D. (1982) *The Minds of Billy Milligan*, New York: Bantam Books. *An account of William Milligan's alleged 23 personalities and his therapy with psychiatrist David Caul.*

Kluft, R.P. (1987) 'First-rank symptoms as a diagnostic clue to multiple personality disorder', *American Journal of Psychiatry*, 144, pp. 293–8.

*Lipton, S. (1943) 'Dissociated personality: a case report', *Psychiatric Quarterly*, 17, pp. 35–6. *Lipton describes the personalities of 'Maud K.' and 'Sara' referred to in the* **Background**.

*Ludwig, A.M., Brandsma, J.M., Wilbur, C.B., Benfeldt, F. & Jameson, D.H. (1972) 'An objective study of multiple personality', *Archives of General Psychiatry*, 26, pp. 298–310. *This award-winning article describes the case of Jonah and his alternate personalities referred to in the* **Background**.

Osgood, C.E., Luria, Z., Jeans, R.E. & Smith, S.W. (1976) 'The three faces of Evelyn: a case report', *Journal of Abnormal Psychology*, 85, pp. 249–70.

*Prince, M. (1905) *The Dissociation of Personality*, New York: Longmans, Green. *This book provides Prince's account of 'Miss Beauchamp' and is probably the first apparent case of MPD to receive serious scientific consideration. Miss Beauchamp may have had as many as 17 distinct personalities*

Schacter, D.L. (1986) 'Amnesia and crime', *American Psychologist*, 41, pp. 186–295.

*Schreiber, F.R. (1973) *Sybil*, Harmondsworth: Penguin. *Schreiber describes the case of an individual with 16 personalities. The film of the same name starred Sally Field.*

*Sizemore, C.C. & Pitillo, E.S. (1977) *I'm Eve*, Garden City, N.Y.: Doubleday. *This is Christine Sizemore's own account of her case of MPD studied by Thigpen & Cleckley (1954, 1957). Evidently, Sizemore split into 22 personalities after apparently being cured.*

Spanos, N.P., Weekes, J.R. & Bertrand, L.D. (1985) 'Multiple personality: A social psychological perspective', *Journal of Abnormal Psychology*, 94, pp. 362–76.

Sue, D., Sue, D. & Sue, S. (1990) *Understanding Abnormal Behaviour*, Boston: Houghton Mifflin.

*Thigpen, C.H. & Cleckley, H.M. (1954) 'A case of multiple personality', *Journal of Abnormal and Social Psychology*, 49, pp. 135–51. *This article describes the case of Christine Sizemore, arguably the most famous case of MPD, and her three personalities 'Eve White', 'Eve Black' and 'Jane' (see also below).*

*Thigpen, C.H. & Cleckley, H.M. (1957) *The Three Faces of Eve*. New York: McGraw-Hill. *This book, a much expanded account of their*

1954 publication, formed the basis for the film of the same name in which Joanne Woodward played the three personalities.

Thigpen, C.H. & Cleckley, H.M. (1984) 'On the incidence of multiple personality disorder', *International Journal of Clinical and Experimental Hypnosis*, 32, pp. 63–6.

3

ARE HOMOSEXUALS BORN AND NOT MADE?

Are homosexuals born and not made?

Simon LeVay
© *The Guardian*

Among the many bizarre notions that Sigmund Freud inflicted on the world, his ideas about male homosexuality must take pride of place.

He asserted that all young boys have a strong sexual bond with their mothers, a bond they have to break in order to develop sexual feelings towards other women. If, on account of the mother's close-binding behaviour, the father's hostility, or other reasons, a boy breaks this bond, as an adult he will seek sexual partners with whom he can re-enact this role – this time taking the mother's part. Although Freud did not write extensively on female sexuality, he seems to have envisaged a mirror-image process to account for it.

Besides lacking supporting evidence, Freud's theory has two unfortunate consequences: first, within a homophobic society, it placed an undeserved burden of guilt on the parents of gays and lesbians. Second, it led to the notion of the 'curability' of homosexuality, a notion with traumatic consequences for many gay men.

Recently, research in various disciplines has been converging on a quite different picture. Neurobiologists have defined the brain circuits responsible for sex behaviour, and have shown that the sexual differentiation of these circuits takes place prenatally under the influence of sex hormones such as testosterone.

Geneticists have demonstrated a strong influence of heredity on sexual orientation in both men and women. Child psychologists have shown that adult homosexuality is to some extent predictable on the basis of childhood characteristics such as gender non-conformity in play. In turn, these childhood characteristics are known from both human and animal studies to be strongly influenced by genetic or hormonal factors operating before birth.

Finally, cognitive scientists have shown that gay men and lesbian women differ from their straight counterparts in a variety of perceptual and behavioural traits – such as verbal skills, and right- or left-handedness – that are most easily explained in terms of differences in prenatal brain development.

In my own research [orginally published in 1991], I described structural differences between gay and straight men in the anterior hypothalamus, the brain region most centrally involved in the production of typical male sex behaviour.

More recently (1992), Laura Allen and Roger Gorski at the University of California, Los Angeles, reported on a second brain difference, this time in the anterior commissure, a pathway connecting the left and right hemispheres of the cerebral cortex. This difference may be related to some of the cognitive differences between gay and straight men mentioned above.

This is not to say we understand what makes people straight or gay. We do not. But the evidence strongly suggests that the factors influencing sexual orientation operate during the normal process of sexual differentiation of the brain, which occurs largely before birth.

Further progress will require the identification of genes that influence sexual orientation. If such genes are found it will be possible to ask when, where and how they exert their effects.

As far as the interests of the gay and lesbian community are concerned, this whole area of research has the potential for both positive and negative consequences. The benefits may include a better understanding of the innate differences between gay and straight people, a rejection of homophobia based on religious or moral arguments, and the extension of greater legal protection to gays and lesbians.

The latter is especially important in countries such as the US where the constitutional protection of groups hinges critically on the demonstration of the 'immutability' of membership in a group. Until now, such protection for gays and lesbians has been rejected by the US courts on the grounds that homosexuality is a 'chosen lifestyle' and hence not immutable.

On the negative side, the current work may reinforce, albeit irrationally, the notion of homosexuality as a defect that can and should be 'fixed', or even prevented by means of prenatal testing and selective abortion. In this connection it should be stressed that science itself has no definition for what is normal, and what is abnormal. Science can only describe what is out there and attempt to explain how it got that way. The acceptance of homosexuality as something normal and desirable depends above all on the image that gays and lesbians themselves present to society.

As a gay man, I believe that I can contribute more to my community by the openness and pride with which I conduct my life than by any amount of laboratory research.

Background

Understanding the reasons why some people have a sexual preference for members of their own sex has long been a topic of psychological interest. The psychodynamic, behavioural, humanistic-existential, and neurobiological perspectives have all offered suggestions about the causal factors that underlie homosexual behaviour, but until recently there has been little firm evidence to support any one theoretical perspective. In 1991, however, Simon LeVay, a British born neurobiologist working at the Salk Institute in California published research (LeVay, 1991) which seemed to indicate quite clearly that the brains of homosexual men were structurally different.

LeVay conducted post-mortem analyses on the brain tissue of 19 homosexual men who had died of an AIDS related illness, 16 men presumed to be heterosexual (six of whom had also died from an AIDS related illness), and six women who were also presumed to be heterosexual. The research concentrated on a cluster of neurons known as the third interstitial nucleus of the anterior hypothalamus (or INAH–3). Typically, this nucleus is around a tenth of a cubic millimetre in volume, and composed of neurons which are similar to those outside it. There does not seem to be a clear border which separates the INAH–3 from other neurons.

It has long been known that, at least in the rat, regions of the hypothalamus are different in males and females, and that these differences are crucial to their sexual behaviour. Drawing on this, and other research indicating that the INAH–3 is bigger in men than women, LeVay proposed that the hypothalamus plays an important role in typical 'masculine' sexuality and that for men the INAH–3 is specifically responsible for engendering sexual interest in women, or what LeVay describes as 'the generation of male-typical sexual behaviour'.

On the basis of these proposals, LeVay predicted that the INAH–3 should be bigger in heterosexual men and homosexual women when compared with homosexual men and heterosexual women. Although LeVay's investigation did not include any female homosexuals, the data indicated that the average size of the INAH–3 amongst male homosexuals and female heterosexuals was much smaller that that of the heterosexual male group. Given these findings, LeVay concluded that it was reasonable to assume that 'sexual orientation has a biological substrate'.

In support of his view that sexual orientation is biologically determined rather than determined by experiences in childhood and adolescence, LeVay has also drawn on research conducted by Laura Allen and Roger Gorski. Allen and Gorski (1992) discovered that the anterior commissure, a neuronal pathway connecting the two cerebral hemispheres was, on average, 34 per cent larger in homosexual men than in their heterosexual counterparts.

Compared with women, the homosexual male anterior commissure was 18 per cent larger, a difference which was statistically non-significant when adjusted for brain-weight differences between men and women. Although this structural difference is not known to be directly involved in sexual behaviour, LeVay has suggested that these findings, coupled with his own, provide 'one more nail in the coffin of critics who argue that heterosexuality is a choice and thus immoral'.

In a recent book detailing his findings, LeVay (1993) has proposed that sexual orientation is established in the womb, as a result of the influence of hormones on the brain of the developing foetus. The idea that animals acquire their 'sex' before birth is not new. In the 1940s, experiments on pregnant laboratory rats indicated that a genetically male foetus would only develop male genitals if the male sex hormones (androgens) were prenatally available. In the absence of prenatal androgens, female internal and external genitalia developed in rats of either sex.

In 1959, Charles Phoenix and his associates (Phoenix, Goy, Gerall & Young, 1959) suggested that sexual behaviour, like the sexual organs, might also be determined before birth by hormones acting on the developing foetus's brain. Phoenix and his colleagues injected testosterone (the primary and most potent androgen) into pregnant guinea pigs. The result was genetically female offspring which had not only developed a penis, but behaved sexually like males, being more likely to try and mount other guinea pigs and less likely to adopt the female sexual posture of arching the back. This finding was replicated by Clemens (1971) who showed that the probability of male-like mounting behaviour was related to the number of brothers in the litter and, presumably, the greater quantity of androgens prenatally available.

The suggestion (e.g. Loraine, Adamopolous, Kirkham, Ismail & Dove, 1971) that homosexual males are lacking in testosterone or have excessive levels of female sex hormones in their blood is now known to be incorrect (e.g. Tourney, 1980) and injecting homosexuals with testosterone does not reduce their homosexual tendencies (Money, 1980). Similarly, female homosexuals do not have lower than normal levels of oestrogen and higher than normal levels of androgens in their bloodstreams (Feder, 1984). However, one hypothesis that has arisen from early hormonal research suggests that inadequate prenatal androgenisation of the brain causes male homosexuality.

The generally accepted model proposes that the 'default program' for the mamalian brain is female. Unless male hormones are available to modify the developing brain when it is particularly open to endocrine influence, a female brain organisation will develop, an idea anticipated by Thomas Aquinas who saw women as '*mas occasionatus*', or men who have not reached their final destination. According to the hypothesis, prenatal androgens exert two effects on sexual behaviour. The first is termed 'masculinisation' and refers to the development of the neural circuits necessary for male sexual behaviour. The second is 'de-feminisation' which refers to the suppression of the development of neural circuits necessary for female sexual behaviour.

Prenatal exposure of the male brain to androgens could produce two effects, masculinisation (which would establish a tendency to perceive females as sexual partners) and de-feminisation (which would suppress the tendency to perceive males as sexual partners). If the hypothesis is correct, then most males would be expected to be exclusively heterosexual as a result of the masculinisation and de-feminisation processes. However, if some factor interfered with the prenatal androgenisation of the developing foetus, then some men would be expected to be bi-sexual (the result of a brain which was masculinised but not de-feminised) and some exclusively homosexual (the result of a brain which was neither masculinised nor de-feminised).

Related to the above are findings which indicate that male and female brains are structurally different. For example, it has been shown in rats that the sexes differ in terms of the number of synaptic connections in the pre-optic area of the hypothalamus, an area known to be of crucial importance in the sex life of males and oestrus cycle of females. In humans too, anatomical sex differences have been reported: the Sexually Dimorphic Nucleus (or INAH–1) is, on average, two and a half times larger in men than women (*New Scientist*, 1992).

For some researchers, the anatomical differences between the sexes determine the way men and women think, and reflect permanent brain alterations caused by differential prenatal exposure to sex hormones. Simon LeVay would argue that the structural brain differences between the sexes, coupled with his own findings, lend strong support to the view that homosexuals are born and not made.

Talking points

1 The structural differences in the anterior hypothalamus of homosexuals and heterosexuals seem to be well established, and the anterior hypothalamus is known to be involved in sexually arousing men to women. However, the research of LeVay and others has not gone unchallenged. What sorts of questions and issues concerning their findings do you think have arisen? It might be helpful to think in terms of measurement, the use of 'average differences', issues of causality, and the samples investigated.

2 If LeVay is correct in his view that homosexuality has a biological basis, then there are enormous implications for ideas of morality, law, politics, and so on. What issues does LeVay see as having important positive consequences for male and female homosexuals? What issues does LeVay see as having negative consequences?

3 If homosexuality is not a mental disorder as, perhaps, most people would agree and as the most recent version of the Diagnostic and Statistical Manual of Mental Disorders (DSM–3–R) acknowledges, then the question of whether homosexuals should receive therapy (which is typically based on aversive conditioning techniques) to change their sexual orientation becomes even more controversial than it already is. As LeVay notes in his article, one consequence of Freud's theory of homosexuality was that it 'led to the notion of the "curability" of [homosexuals] with traumatic consequences for many gay men'.

According to Davison (1978), the very existence of 'sexual reorientation' treatment programs strengthens prejudice against homosexuals. In Davison's view the only ethical course is to stop offering this type of treatment even to those who voluntarily seek it. What are your views on this issue? Do you think that homosexuals who seek 'treatment' should have a 'right' to receive it?

4 As LeVay's article notes, research has shown that adult homosexuality 'is to some extent predictable on the basis of childhood characteristics such as gender nonconformity', and that such characteristics are known to be strongly influenced by genetic or hormonal factors operating prenatally. What sorts of behaviours would constitute gender nonconformity in boys and girls? Why do you think gender nonconformity isn't a complete predictor of adult homosexuality, and why does this weaken LeVay's argument for a biological basis to homosexuality? Note that the data concerning gender nonconformity in play derive from adults' self-reports of their childhood years. What are the dangers of relying on self-report measures?

5 LeVay notes that 'geneticists have demonstrated a strong influence of heredity on sexual orientation in both men and women'. Kallmann (1952) reported a 100 per cent concordance rate for homosexuality in 40 pairs of identical or monozygotic (MZ) twins as compared with less than 15 per cent in non-identical or dizygotic (DZ) twins. Pillard and Weinrich (1986) have reported a four-fold increase above expectancy for male siblings of male homosexuals. Indeed, it has recently been claimed by Dean Hamer and his colleagues (Hamer, Hu, Magnuson, Hu & Pattatucci, 1993) that there is some evidence to implicate a region of the X chromosome (called Xq28), which a man inherits from his mother, in the sexual orientation of some gay men (though note that this is *not* to suggest that a 'gay gene' has been discovered).

Although such studies seem to offer strong support for the influence of heredity on sexual orientation, why do they not definitively support a genetic explanation? If homosexuality can be identified as the expression of a normally functioning gene then, irrespective of whether the gene acts on hormones, homosexuality could be said to have received a 'Darwinian blessing' (Kohn, 1992). Although it is unlikely that a gene inhibiting reproduction would survive, can you think of a way in which it might be possible to account for its apparently paradoxical existence?

6 Sigmund Freud is identified in LeVay's article as having offered an explanation for homosexuality. According to Freud, the homosexual male is unable to **a)** overcome his strong attachment to his mother, **b)** identify with his father, and consequently **c)** proceed to the mature stage of genital sexuality, seeking partners of the opposite sex. Freud terms this 'faulty resolution of the Oedipus complex'.

The strong attachment to the mother is held to stem from what has been termed the 'smother mother' syndrome, in which the mother is domineering, physically intimate, and close binding. Non-identification with the father is held to stem from his cold, unaffectionate, and even hostile behaviour towards the child. Lacking an adequate male figure on which to base his behaviour, and experiencing 'castration anxiety', the male child continues to seek male affection never given by his father and avoids contact with female genitalia for fear of injury to or loss of his penis. For Freud, homosexuality develops as a substitute for the heterosexual adaptation that the individual's fears prevent him from achieving, but for which he still yearns at some level (Bieber, 1976).

Whilst LeVay sees Freud's theory as 'a bizarre notion ... [lacking] supportive evidence', support for it has been claimed. Bieber (1976) describes an earlier (1962) study in which male homosexuals receiving psychotherapy were interviewed about their childhoods. The interviews revealed a frequent occurrence of family backgrounds which fitted the 'classic pattern'. As interesting as such data are, at least two findings would argue against a Freudian interpretation. What would these findings be? What kinds of criticisms would you make of the sample interviewed by Bieber, and the method Bieber used to collect his data?

As LeVay notes, 'Freud did not write extensively on female sexuality [although] he seems to have envisaged a mirror image process to account for it'. What would this 'mirror image' process be? More generally, if in the absence of any evidence it can be claimed that homosexuality stems from an unhappy childhood, what two other claims could also legitimately be made?

7 The social learning perspective suggests that homosexuality could be a learned preference. If sexual interaction during adolescence or early adulthood with a member of the same sex is pleasurable, it may induce homosexual orientation through positive reinforcement. Alternatively, heterosexual behaviour could be conditioned to become an aversive stimulus. What other circumstances would a social learning theorist see as potential causal factors for the development of homosexuality? What sorts of research findings do you think would argue against a behavioural perspective?

8 LeVay suggests that homo- and heterosexual men and women have been shown to differ 'in a variety of perceptual and behavioural traits such as verbal skills and right- or left-handedness', and that these are 'most easily explained in terms of prenatal brain development', a view with which at least some cognitive psychologists would agree. In what cognitive abilities are heterosexual men and women held to be different, and what predictions would be made about the abilities of homosexuals given these differences? Why do you think LeVay should implicate 'handedness' as an important difference between homosexuals and heterosexuals?

References and further reading

Those references which are particularly worthy of further reading are indicated thus: * , together with a brief description of their area of concern.

*Allen, L. & Gorski, R. (1992) 'Sexual orientation and the size of the anterior commissure in the human brain', *Proceedings of the National Academy of Science*, 89, pp. 7199–202. *Allen and Gorski's measurements of the cross-sectional area of the anterior commissure in homosexual men and heterosexual men and women are presented in this article.*

Bieber, I.A. (1976) 'Discussion of "Homosexuality: The ethical challenge"', *Journal of Consulting and Clinical Psychology*, 44, pp. 163–6.

Clemens, L.G. (1971) 'Influence of prenatal litter composition on mounting behaviour of female rats', *American Zoologist*, 11, pp. 617–18.

*Davison, G.C. (1978) 'Not can but ought: the treatment of homosexuality', *Journal of Consulting and Clinical Psychology*, 46, pp. 170–2. *This article considers some of the ethical issues surrounding the 'treatment' of homosexuality.*

Feder, H.H. (1984) 'Hormones and sexual behaviour', *Annual Review of Psychology*, 35, pp. 165–200.

*Hamer, D.H., Hu, S., Magnuson, V., Hu, N. & Pattatucci, A.M. (1993) 'A linkage between DNA markers on the X chromosome and male sexual orientation', *Science*, 261, pp. 321–7. *Hamer and his associates' evidence for an apparent chromosomal inheritance shared by a group of homosexual brothers is detailed in this article.*

Kallman, F.J. (1952) 'Twin and sibship study of overt male homosexuality', *American Journal of Human Genetics*, 4, pp. 136–46.

Kohn, M. (1992) 'Sex and the brain', *New Statesman and Society*, 27 November, pp. 31–2.

*LeVay, S. (1991) 'A difference in hypothalamic structure between heterosexual and homosexual men', *Science*, 254, pp. 1034–7. *LeVay's measurements of the volume of INAH–3 in heterosexual men and women and homosexual men is presented in this article.*

*LeVay, S. (1993) *The Sexual Brain*, Boston, Massachusetts: MIT Press. *LeVay's book summarises in an accessible way the available evidence concerning the biological basis of homosexuality.*

Loraine, J.A., Adamopolous, D.A., Kirkham, E.E., Ismail, A.A. & Dove, G.A. (1971) 'Patterns of hormone excretion in male and female homosexuals', *Nature*, 234, pp. 552–5.

Money, J. (1980) *Love and Love Sickness*, Baltimore: Johns Hopkins University Press.

**New Scientist* (1992) 'Obscure origins of desire', published as a supplement to *New Scientist*, 28 November. *This supplement provides an excellent review of research linking the development of the brain to sexual behaviour.*

Phoenix, C.H., Goy, R.W., Gerall, A.A. & Young, W.C. (1959) 'Organizing action of prenatally administered testosterone propionate on the tissues mediating mating behaviour in the guinea pig', *Endocrinology*, 65, pp. 369–82.

Pillard, R.C. & Weinrich, J.A. (1986) 'Evidence of familial nature of male homosexuality', *Archives of General Psychiatry*, 43, pp. 808–12.

Tourney, G. (1980) 'Hormones and homosexuality', **in** J. Marmor (Ed.), *Homosexual Behaviour*, New York: Basic Books.

4

A TWIN PEEK AT FAMILY FORTUNES

A twin peek at family fortunes

© Jerome Burne
The Times
14/1/93

One of the marks of a model family is the mountain of toys and books designed to boost the children into the educational fast lane. But does encouragement make any difference or do children arrive with pre-programmed limits?

Acting as educational cheerleaders may not make much difference according to Dr Sandra Scarr, of Virginia University and the president of the Society for Research in Child Development. She says that 'identical twins who are separated at birth and brought up in quite different homes end up with very similar personalities and IQ'.

Findings like that are reviving the old debate about nature versus nurture, but this time it has been given a new twist by researchers such as Dr Scarr who believe that rather than being the passive victims of our environment, we are driven by our genes to create our own environment.

Rationing television time or peddling poetry rather than mountain bikes will not change the way our children turn out. Recently, several researchers have reported findings that begin to build up a picture of just which bits of our character and behaviour are inherited and which

[are] more susceptible to change.

Identical twins, especially when they are separated at birth, are the key to teasing out the complex links between genes and behaviour. Because each one has the same genetic pattern, it is possible to see how quite different environments affect exactly the same set of genes.

Take, for example, intelligence. When identical twins are tested for intelligence, they get very similar scores but when their brothers and sisters in the same family are tested, on average they come out only half as similar. On a scale of nought to one, twins come out at about 0.75 and brothers and sisters at 0.4.

The same sort of tests and calculations can be done for almost anything from height and weight to being good at maths or interested in woodwork. When you get a high score for identical twins and a low score or zero for non-identical brothers and sisters, you have a feature strongly controlled by genes and therefore hard to change.

Dr David Lykken, a director of a large-scale study at Minnesota University of twins reared apart, has developed the paradoxical-sounding theory of inherited characteristics that do not run in families.

The familiar picture is that because siblings share their parents' genes, they will share their qualities to a greater or lesser extent. But there are some abilities and interests that identical twins will both have very strongly but which other members of the family show no signs of at all, suggesting that they are strongly genetically controlled. What we now believe, Dr Lykken says, is that many complex traits, such as leadership, artistic ability, selling ability, genius and even parenting are genetically controlled.

In the past the genetic element in these talents has been ignored because they don't run in families. For example, Dr Lykken's team has found

that an interest in both gambling and blood sports was quite strongly influenced by environmental factors. Identical twins in a family that had no interest in casinos or hunting were not much more likely to sneak off to put £5 on the 3.20 than their non-identical brothers and sisters. On the other hand, an interest in arts and crafts had a strong genetic basis.

Just in, but as yet unpublished, are results that suggest that authoritarian conservatives can no more help their views than the determined wood carver can give up the chisel. 'The authoritarian personality is a very well-established type' Dr Lykken says. 'We found identical twins had a very high correlation of 0.7 on it while brothers or sisters raised apart from their families had zero correlation.'

What does all this mean for the bewildered parent? 'It might make people more sensitive to the fact that their children may have abilities they haven't even dreamt of' Dr Lykken says.

'It should also make parents more relaxed. In the long night of the environmentalists, the idea that every child had the same potential meant that every parent was a failure if their child didn't turn out a success.'

This message is echoed by Dr Jim Stevenson, of the behavioural science unit at the Institute of Child Health in London. At a recent conference he reported that social behaviour – being outgoing and interested in other people – seems to be strongly genetic, while antisocial behaviour – lying, cheating and bullying – are much more influenced by family life. So it is largely a waste of time pressurising children to socialise, but it is well worth encouraging them always to be truthful.

Dr Stevenson believes he has uncovered similar guidelines for other aspects of child rearing. 'Hyperactivity and poor concentration span are strongly genetic' he says. 'On the other hand, reading has bits that are easy to change and bits that aren't. Linking letters with sound is much more genetically controlled than recognising words as units, so concentrate on one and not the other.'

What happens, Dr Scarr and others believe, is that children's genes drive them to create their own personal environment. Right from birth, brothers and sisters bring out different responses from people; unattractive or shy ones – both strongly genetic traits – will be treated differently from attractive, outgoing ones.

'It seems that it is the unique things that happen to children – having a serious illness, getting on really well or very badly with one teacher – that can have more impact on their development than the regularities of home life. This is especially true of social development' Dr Stevenson says.

None of the gene believers are saying that environment does not matter.

'Parents can make a great difference to a child's sense of ambition or self-esteem' Dr Scarr says.

'But the evidence from identical twins raised in different families, and the fact that children raised in adoptive families from birth show no correlation of intelligence or personality with other members of the family, tells parents they should not worry if they go to the ball game or the museum with their children.'

Background

It is widely believed that abilities of various kinds appear to run in families. What is more arguable is why this may be so. One of psychology's most enduring controversies concerns the relative importance of heredity and environment in human development. Known by psychologists as the nature–nurture debate and by philosophers as the nativism–empirism controversy, the debate originally turned on questions of innate qualities of mind that were assumed to be universal and found in all non-pathological instances (Reber, 1985). Philosophers like Plato and Descartes, for example, believed that humans are born with at least some ideas, such as the axioms of geometry. Other philosophers such as Aristotle, Locke and Hume believed that humans are born without knowledge of specific ideas and that all thoughts develop in some way or another from experience of the world (Wertheimer, 1970).

The debate concerning the origins of capacities which are universal has certainly been vigorous. The nature–nurture debate has, however been most controversial when applied to a consideration of the differences between individuals. Researchers have used a number of methodological approaches to try and resolve the nature–nurture debate. The most obvious approach has been to look for similarities within families with respect to the characteristic of interest.

In a very early study, Sir Francis Galton (1869) traced the family trees of nearly 1 000 'eminent people' including judges, politicians, scientists, artists, religious leaders and scholars. Galton believed that Darwin's principle of natural selection held for the inheritance of certain human psychological characteristics as well as various morphological characteristics of other species. Galton claimed that certain stigmatic qualities as well as desirable qualities tended to run in families. This led him to propose a programme of eugenics, in which humans would selectively breed in order to improve the stock of homo sapiens.

Whilst it is generally accepted that Galton's work tells us little if anything about the inheritance of psychological characterisics, his pioneering research helped to establish other important methodological approaches. One strategy deriving from Galton's work is the study of adopted children. If a characteristic is determined or strongly affected by genetic factors, adopted children should resemble their biological parents more than their adoptive parents. If, however, the environment is the key determinant of a characteristic, the adopted children should resemble their adoptive parents. In the area of intelligence, for example, some studies have claimed support for the nativist position (e.g. Jencks, 1972; Munsinger, 1978). However, other studies have failed to support it; indeed, at least one study has shown that the IQs of adopted children become increasingly similar to those of their adoptive parents over time (Scarr & Weinberg, 1977).

Another strategy that researchers use is the examination of monozygotic twins, the argument being that if a characteristic is determined by heredity, the more closely two people are genetically related, the more similar they should be with respect to the characteristic. Since monozygotic twins share identical sets of chromosomes, they are genetically identical. They would therefore be expected to be very similar with respect to a characteristic, if that characteristic was determined or strongly affected by genetic factors.

In what is widely considered to be a classic article, Erlenmeyer-Kimling and Jarvik (1963) summarised the evidence regarding IQ resemblances between biological and adoptive relatives. Fifty-two studies conducted in eight countries and using more than 30 000 people revealed a number of consistent results. Thus, the similarity of IQs between parents and children and brothers and sisters was greater than that between half-siblings which was in turn greater than that between cousins. The most important finding, however, was that monozygotic twins raised in the same family were most similar with respect to their IQs and more closely related than dizygotic twins of the same sex who were similarly raised. Since the major difference between these twin types is that monozygotic twins are genetically identical whilst dizygotic twins are no more closely related than any pair of siblings, the findings were taken as strong support for the role of genetic factors in intelligence. Subsequent studies have confirmed this finding and have led to the conclusion that 'genes are the major systematic force influencing the development of individual differences in IQ' (Plomin & De Fries, 1980).

The high degree of similarity between identical twins raised in the same environment is not entirely unexpected. Much more convincing would be evidence of similarity between identical twins who had been separated either at birth or very early in life, and who have been raised in different environments. Such 'experiments in nature' (Hassett & White, 1989) are rare. In the area of intelligence the first reported study was conducted by Newman, Freeman and Holzinger (1937). They studied 19 pairs of twins who had been reared apart and reported some degree of similarity in their IQ scores.

Between 1955 and 1966, the British Psychologist Sir Cyril Burt published several reports which seemed to suggest that the similarity in IQ scores of monozygotic twins reared apart was actually very high, and higher than that for dizygotic twins of the same sex reared together. However, Burt's research was challenged, particularly by Kamin (1977) who pointed out some remarkable consistencies in Burt's work which were so improbable that the possibility of intentional data fabrication had to be considered.

Further investigations of Burt's studies revealed that in addition to the likelihood that his data were fabricated, it was also possible that he had falsified the names of supposed co-researchers (Hearnshaw, 1979). The scandal concerning Burt did much to harm psychology in general and twin research in particular. However, there are several other studies comparing the similarity of IQ of monozygotic twins reared apart in which data fabrication is not a consideration. In one of these, Shields (1962) reported data based on 40 pairs of identical twins which were very similar to those Burt is alleged to have fabricated.

At present there are several research programmes looking at the role of genetic factors in psychological characteristics. The most elaborate of these is the Minnesota Study of Twins Reared Apart headed by Thomas Bouchard jnr. (e.g. Bouchard, 1987). For over a decade more than 100 identical twins who were separated early in life and raised in different homes have been studied. The research has attempted to provide what is known as a heritability estimate for various psychological characteristics. Although genes are a biochemical blueprint for development, there are many other factors which affect development, and the way genes are expressed always depends to some extent on the environment (this is why the question, 'Is intelligence inherited?' is misleading since the answer depends on the group that is studied and the environment in which they were raised: Hassett & White, 1989).

Heritability is a mathematical estimate of the relative importance of genetics and the environment in determining a particular trait for a specific population. It does not provide a statement of how much of a characteristic is attributable to genes, but only a statement about the separating out of the variability due to genetic or environmental factors. The Minnesota team have claimed that about 70 per cent of the variance in IQ test scores and 50 per cent of personality differences is accounted for by genetic factors. The research findings have generated much interest not least because of other unusual similarities that have been observed in reunited twins. These include being habitual gigglers, always wearing seven rings and even always entering the sea backwards and then only to the knees!

Talking points

1 The debate over the influence of 'nature' and 'nurture' in determining the course of human development is not new, and on first inspection the framework for the debate is relatively straightforward. As noted in the **Background**, nativists see the cause (and therefore the course) of human development as being determined by innate factors, that is, a consequence of genetic factors. Empirists, on the other hand, see experience as determining the course of human development. Given its apparent straightforwardness, why do you think that most psychologists now consider nature versus nurture to be a largely outdated debate?

2 Identical twins are one of the basic 'tools' of psychologists interested in studying the role of heredity in the determination of psychological characteristics. According to the article, 'identical twins who are separated at birth and brought up in quite different homes end up with very similar personalities and IQ'. What alternative explanation or explanations could you offer for this finding which may make the acceptance of a genetic hypothesis a premature (and indeed confounded) conclusion? What methodological cautions do you believe should always be exercised in twin studies?

3 According to the article, 'when identical twins are tested for intelligence, they get very similar scores but when their brothers and sisters in the same family are tested, on average they come out only half as similar. On a scale of nought to one, twins come out at about 0.75 and brothers and sisters at 0.4 . . . When you get a high score for identical twins and a low score or zero for non-identical brothers and sisters, you have a feature strongly controlled by genes and therefore hard to change.' The article does not explain what these figures mean, other than suggesting that they are some measure of similarity and therefore comparability. What do you think the figures could possibly be? How would you temper the author's apparent enthusiasm over the importance of the figures that are quoted?

4 The use of correlation in the nature–nurture debate is often used to overstate the position of one argument at the expense of the other. Correlations, however, do not imply causation. Two variables may be accidentally correlated by virtue of a complex and interactive correlation with a third (or even more) variable. Additionally, correlation merely measures the nature and extent of co-variance. Only an experiment may indicate a causal relationship between variables (and even then the causal relationship is based on a specified level of confidence in statistical terms that the results were not due to random error or chance). If you wanted to examine the role of genetic and environmental factors for a psychological characteristic, how would you design an experiment to overcome the inferential limitations of the correlational approach?

5 Although the article does not address psychological disorders, recent developments in molecular biology have suggested that there may be a link between genes and a variety of mental disorders. For example, Egeland and Hostetter (1983) have studied the Amish community in Pennsylvania, North America. Although the sample sizes were small, the claim was made that there are specific marker genes located on chromosome 11 which are present in those members of the Amish who suffer from manic-depression. Despite only 63 per cent 'penetrance' of the gene (which means that 37 per cent of those who had the markers did not suffer manic-depression), it has been suggested that the genetic markers on chromosome 11 can put people 'at risk' of manic-depression (Egeland, Gerhard, Pauls, Sussex, Kidd, Allen, Hostetter & Housman, 1987). How do you think an environmentalist would counter the claim that genetic factors may be responsible for the manic-depressive disorder?

6 As noted above, research using family concordance techniques similar to those which have investigated the potential origins of manic-depression, has looked at the possible genetic basis for schizophrenia. Bouchard's Minnesota team have uncovered remarkable similarities in the characteristics of identical twins reared apart. These have led to the generation of models indicating the relative probabilities for the genetic transmission of the disorder (e.g. McGue, Gottesman & Rao, 1985). Other research (e.g. Iversen, 1979) has linked the experience of schizophrenia with abnormally high levels of the neurotransmitter dopamine. It is not clear whether high levels of dopamine cause schizophrenia or whether the experience of schizophrenia causes high levels of dopamine, or even if the link is at all causal. Notwithstanding these cautions, how could genes and neurotransmitters interact to produce disorders like schizophrenia?

7 Recent re-investigations of personality traits using factor analysis have discovered a small number of robust, possibly universal, personality factors which account for most of the total variability in behaviour. Such factors have also been argued to be genetically influenced. For example, using twin studies again, the broad heritability of the major personality dimensions of extroversion–introversion and neuroticism–stability is about 50 per cent (Eysenck, 1990). Furthermore, a review conducted by Zuckerman (1991) indicates a similar level of heritability for the 'psychoticism–impulsive unsocialised sensation seeking conglomerate' (Deary & Matthews, 1993). In what ways do you think problems of measuring and assessing personality could contribute to the limitations of these findings?

8 The interaction of genetic and environmental factors may be seen with a disorder called phenylketonuria (PKU). This disorder involves the inheritance of two recessive genes, one from each parent, which prevents the body from producing an enzyme that metabolises phenylalanine (a common constituent of many foodstuffs, particularly dairy produce). If untreated, phenylalanine builds up in the bloodstream, causing poisoning, severe mental retardation and eventually death (Gross, 1992). However, by placing an affected child on a low protein diet for the first 12 years, these effects can be prevented and normal development occurs. How could you apply this 'interactive' effect between genes and the environment to other psychological characteristics?

9 Haier, Siegel, Neuchterlein, Hazlett, Wu, Peak and Browning (1988) have used 'positron emission tomography' to study the human brain whilst various tasks are being attempted. The researchers reported a strong link between scores on the Raven's advanced progressive matrices (held to be some measure of intelligence) and level of brain activity. What is especially surprising is the fact that the link is negative: high scorers on the measure of intelligence showed lower brain activity than low scorers. In some cases, activity was twice as high in the brains of low scorers than high scorers. Can these findings be taken as support for the view that intelligence stems at least in part from genetic factors, and how would you explain the inverse link?

10 The challenge of future research is now to examine carefully the impact of gene–environment interactions for a range of characteristics, abilities, disorders, and achievements and to view the effectiveness of intervention programmes in each area within the total context of the interactional analysis. What areas not mentioned here or in the article do you see as particularly ripe for further research?

References and further reading

Those references which are particularly worthy of further reading are indicated thus: *, together with a brief description of their area of concern.

*Bouchard, T.J., Jr. (1987) *Information about the Minnesota Center for Twin and Adoption Research*, Minneapolis: University of Minnesota. *This provides some details about the work Bouchard and his colleagues are undertaking.*

Deary, I.J. & Matthews, G. (1993) 'Personality traits are alive and well', *The Psychologist*, 6, pp. 299–311.

Egeland, J.A. & Hostetter, A.M. (1983) 'Amish Study, 1: affective disorders among the Amish, 1976–1980', *American Journal of Psychiatry*, 140, pp. 56–61.

*Egeland, J.A., Gerhard, D.S., Pauls, D.L., Sussex, J.N., Kidd, K.K., Allen, C.R., Hostetter, A.M. & Houseman, D.E. (1987) 'Bipolar affective disorders linked to DNA markers on Chromosome 11', *Nature*, 325, pp. 785–7. *Although the claims made by the researchers have subsequently been withdrawn on methodological grounds, this paper was the catalyst for later analyses of gene–environment interactions which remain under investigation.*

*Erlenmeyer-Kimling, L. & Jarvik, L.F. (1963) 'Genetics and intelligence', *Science*, 142. pp. 1477–9. *A classic article providing an early summary of the available evidence concerning similarities in IQ among different family members.*

*Eysenck, H.J. (1990) 'Genetic and environmental contributions to individual differences: the three major dimensions of personality', *Journal of Personality*, 58, pp. 245–61. *An excellent review article written with typical conviction.*

Galton, F. (1869) *Hereditary Genius: An Inquiry into its Laws and Consequences*, London: Macmillan.

Gross, R.D. (1992) *Psychology: The Science of Mind and Behaviour*, London: Hodder & Stoughton.

Haier, R.J., Siegel, B.V., Jr., Neuchterlein, K.H., Hazlett, E., Wu, J.C., Paek, J., Browning, H.L. & Buschsbaum, M.S. (1988) 'Cortical glucose metabolic rate correlates of abstract reasoning and attention studied with positron emission tomography', **cited in** Baron, R.A. (1989) *Psychology: The Essential Science*, London: Allyn & Bacon.

Hassett, J. & White, K.M. (1989) *Psychology in Perspective*, New York: Harper & Row.

Hearnshaw, L.S. (1979) *Cyril Burt, Psychologist*, New York: Cornell University Press.

Iverson, L.L. (1979) 'The chemistry of the brain', *Scientific American*, 241, pp. 134–49.

Jencks, D. (1972) *Inequality: A Reassessment of the Effect of the Family and Schooling in America*, New York: Basic Books.

*Kamin, L.J. (1977) *The Science and Politics of IQ*, Harmondsworth: Penguin. *An examination of apparent fraud in the work of Sir Cyril Burt, containing some clever psychological detective work.*

McGue, M., Gottesman, I.I. & Rao, D.C. (1985) 'Resolving genetic models for the transmission of schizophrenia', *Genetic Epidemiology*, 2, pp. 99–110.

Munsinger, H.A. (1978) 'The adopted child's IQ: a crucial review', *Psychological Bulletin*, 82, pp. 623–59.

Newman, H.H., Freeman, F.N. & Holzinger, K.J. (1937) *Twins: A Study of Heredity and the Environment*, Chicago: University of Chicago Press.

Plomin, R. & De Fries, J.C. (1980) 'Genetics and intelligence: Recent data', *Intelligence*, 4, pp. 15–24.

Reber, A.S. (1985) *The Penguin Dictionary of Psychology*, Harmondsworth: Penguin.

Scarr, S. & Weinberg, R.A. (1977) 'IQ test performance of black children adopted by white families', *American Psychologist*, 31, pp. 726–39.

Shields, J. (1962) *Monozygotic Twins Brought Up Apart and Brought Up Together*, Oxford: Oxford University Press.

Wertheimer, M. (1970) *A Brief History of Psychology*, New York: Holt, Rinehart & Winston.

Zuckerman, M. (1991) *Psychobiology of Personality*, Cambridge: Cambridge University Press.

5

FANATICAL GURU OF BEHAVIORISM

Fanatical guru of behaviourism

Stuart Sutherland
© *The Guardian*
21/8/90

B.F. Skinner was the last of the behaviourists, or at least the last of any note. He was also the most extreme. He achieved fame among some and notoriety among others by his repeated assertion that all behaviour is explainable solely in terms of genetic predispositions and 'reinforcements'; the latter is the technical term for rewards and punishments.

The sheer simplicity of this theory attracted many disciples. To predict what a person would do next, all one needs to know is the history of the reinforcement to which he has been subjected. Such mental terms as 'percepts, thoughts, intentions, abilities, instincts, daydreams, joy, compassion, beliefs' (extracted from a much longer list given by Skinner), have no place in the explanation of behaviour and indeed have no meaning except in so far as they are tied to behaviour.

It is only too easy to demonstrate the inadequacy of Skinner's views. If a sharp electric shock is delivered to someone every time a buzzer sounds, he will come to fear the buzzer. The fear is evinced both as behavioural responses, for example, sweating, and as a subjective feeling, but it receives no reward whatever; indeed, if anything, the response is punished.

Again, Noam Chomsky has pointed out that if someone enjoys reading one of Skinner's books, he has been reinforced and should therefore read it a second time. Skinner could reply that reading a book a second time is not the same response as reading it the first time, but

such a reply would undermine his own theory. When a pleasurable event occurs, we interpret both the event and the responses that led to it; whether an action is repeated depends on these interpretations, which are of course determined by cognitive factors. The influence of reinforcement depends less on what a person does than on what he believes he is doing.

It is here that Skinner's simple-minded theory breaks down. Without taking into account a person's thoughts it is impossible to know what response he is making. A rat taught to press a bar with its foot in order to gain food will sit on the bar if its forefeet are tied together. Even Skinner admitted that a response is not a set of muscular movements, but he never faced the question of how one can know what response is being made. The attempt to explain behaviour without acknowledging internal factors was bound to fail: it is as though a chemist were to try to explain the behaviour of a molecule without reference to its internal structure.

Why is it, then, that Skinner is currently the psychologist who is best known to the general public and why was he so eminent in learned circles?

First, he was a fanatic. He repeated the same simple message over and over again: all that matters is the way in which behaviour is reinforced. Fanatics come to be believed, particularly if they have, as was true of Skinner, a good prose style and oral delivery, and are completely convinced of their righteousness. Second, early in life, he made one important discovery; if an organism is rewarded for making a response on only some of the occasions it does so, and if the reward is then never given at all, the animal will take much longer to stop making the response completely than one that was originally rewarded on every occasion. Third, he invented an ingenious automatic method of reinforcing and recording responses, the celebrated Skinner box. In its simplest form it contains a lever and a panel that can be illuminated. The rat or pigeon learns to press the lever in order to obtain

automatic delivery of food. The apparatus delighted other experimenters: since the recording of the lever presses was entirely automatic, the results could not be influenced by the experimenters expectations. Moreover, once the experiment was set up, the experimenter could scarper off to drink cups of coffee or play noughts and crosses with his colleagues. However, the Skinner box has its drawbacks. There is not much an animal can do in it except press the bar. Indeed, it has been described as a bloodless method of decerebrating the animal. Some think the same could be said of the effects of Skinnerian theory on his adherents.

But perhaps of more importance was a further message in which Skinner persisted. He argued that it was possible to control everybody's behaviour by applying rewards and punishments in the right way: in his novel, *Walden Two*, he gives a portrait of Utopia brought about by the application of such methods. He advocated their use in the classroom and in the treatment of the mentally ill.

It is true that behavioural methods have had some success with certain forms of mental illness, particularly phobias, but even here the methods used derive not from Skinner's theory but from his august predecessor, Pavlov. Mental patients can be induced to behave better (though not to feel better) by rewarding them for dressing decently, eating properly, washing themselves and so on. But there are two problems. When they leave the hospital and the rewards can no longer be given, they go back to their old ways. Moreover, such methods can only be applied within an institution – it is impossible to impose a 'schedule of reinforcement' on anyone at all free, a word that was anathema to Skinner.

Skinner on occasion practised his methods on himself. On visiting his office, I recall noticing a pen automatically drawing a line on a chart above his desk. He explained that it went slowly upwards whenever his desk light was on, and the steadily rising curve reinforced him for working, though from two flat patches I inferred that he had recently taken a couple of holidays. His self-reinforcement was, however, not always so efficacious. When he visited me in Oxford, I took him up Magdalen College tower, but he refused to emerge from the stairs on to the roof, for he suffered from acrophobia. His wife had not even risked the stairs, for she was claustrophobic. Behaviour control is not always as simple as Skinner claims.

Skinner was, then, a man who promised more than he could fulfil, both in his theorising and in its applications. Some of his early work was important, but it can be argued that once he became the guru of psychology he severely held up progress in the subject. His disciples are a dwindling band, for in the changing fashions of psychology, 'behaviourism' has long been replaced by its antonym, 'cognitive science', a movement that Skinner fought until his death with his customary tenacity and ferocity.

Background

Burrhus (his mother's maiden name) Frederic Skinner was born in Susquehanna, Pennsylvania, on March 20th 1904. When he graduated from Hamilton College in New York State in 1926, Skinner was initially determined to pursue a literary career. However, after an unsuccessful period of writing that he called his 'Dark Year', he embarked on graduate studies in psychology at Harvard University, even though he had not previously studied the discipline.

After receiving his MA in 1930 and his PhD in 1931, Skinner was appointed first as National Research Council Fellow at Harvard (1931–1933) and then Junior Fellow of the Harvard Society of Fellows (1933–1936). During his time at Harvard, Skinner became, in his own words, a 'complete behaviourist' and was 'shocked' when people used 'mentalistic' terms. Following the key principles laid down by Watson (1930) Skinner argued that psychology should be the rigorous and scientific study of behaviour, and that this could only be achieved by examining direct, observable evidence. Skinner thus rejected earlier mentalism on the grounds that it was unobservable and unreliable. Whilst he believed that it was possible to be a behaviourist *and* recognise the existence of conscious events, Skinner argued that if psychology was to be scientific its concepts must be defined *as if* they did not refer to a 'private world'.

Early on in his work, Skinner distinguished between two types of learning. One of these is termed 'respondent conditioning' in which learnt behaviour is simply a response (an increase or decrease in a behaviour) following an environmental stimulus. Respondent conditioning is better known as 'classical' conditioning, the principles of which were extensively researched by Ivan Pavlov (1927). Skinner called the other type of learning 'operant conditioning'. This is when an organism learns to behave in a particular way (or 'operate' on its environment) in order to achieve a particular outcome. Skinner used the term 'reinforcer' to describe those outcomes which lead to a behaviour increasing in frequency. An outcome which leads to a behaviour decreasing in frequency is called a 'punisher'.

Classical conditioning involves associating an involuntary response (that is, a response which is not under direct conscious control such as salivation) with some stimulus (such as a bell) that initially did not trigger it. The early behaviourists suggested that this simple form of learning could form the basis of more complex behaviour. Skinner disagreed since he felt that most of what we do could only be explained by operant learning. Operant conditioning is not a simple stimulus–response association like classical conditioning. Rather, it is an association between environmental cues and a behaviour. These could, for example, be the presence of a lever that has in the past produced food when pressed, and the actual pressing of that lever. Skinner saw operant conditioning as being more important than classical conditioning since most of an organism's actions are under voluntary control.

A large amount of Skinner's work involved the operant conditioning of rats and pigeons in specially constructed boxes which his colleagues termed 'Skinner boxes' (though Skinner himself did not like the term). The results of his early research were published in 1938 in a book entitled *The Behaviour of Organisms*. The book was not without its critics. As one reviewer wrote, 'Experiments with white rats are certainly not enough to establish a system of behaviour. A better title would be "Properties of Certain Specific Complex Reflex Mechanisms in the White Rat" '.

When his first book was published Skinner had left Harvard and joined the University of Minnesota where he remained until 1945. From 1945 to 1948 he was Professor and Chairman of the psychology department at Indiana University. As a result of further research Skinner described a range of general learning principles (see, for example, Ferster & Skinner, 1957). One important feature he examined was the effect of varying how often and how predictably reinforcers are given. Surprisingly, under certain conditions infrequent and unpredictable reinforcers can produce stronger (more frequent) behaviour than continuous reinforcement.

This is particularly shown when reinforcement is stopped. If the previous reinforcers were infrequent and unpredictable, the behaviour falls off (or 'extinguishes') more slowly than if they were frequent and predictable. Skinner also looked at the relative effectiveness of reinforcement and punishment. He suggested that punishment was relatively ineffective since it simply suppressed an existing behaviour instead of developing a new behaviour. The old (undesirable) behaviour was liable to return (or 'spontaneously recover') when the punishment was stopped. Thus, he saw reinforcement as being most effective in promoting desirable behaviour.

Skinner applied these general principles in his second book published in 1948. *Walden Two* was a novel, and described Skinner's vision of a Utopia. In this Utopia, behaviour was the outcome of early learning experiences. Through expert child care and educational technology, society would 'shape' the behaviour of its members and transmit its culture effectively. Skinner argued that this would make human life as pleasant and painless as possible. By rewarding good behaviour and reconditioning those who displayed deviant behaviour, the citizens of Skinner's Utopia would 'behave well, productively, and creatively for positive reasons'.

In 1948 Skinner returned to Harvard University as Professor until 1974 and Professor Emeritus thereafter. Amongst other things Skinner also applied his ideas to education, developing a behaviouristic approach using linear programmes of instruction (1968). Less successfully, he attempted to explain general language development (1957) believing it to occur as the result of the reinforcement of spontaneous and imitated speech acts.

Skinner's most controversial book was published in 1971. In *Beyond*

Freedom and Dignity he suggested that behaviour is entirely the product of a conditioning history and a genetic (or inherited biological) potential. For Skinner, 'behaviour is shaped and maintained by its consequences' and people should not object 'when a scientific analysis traces their behaviour to external conditions'. This rejects the very notion of free will and the sense that humans should be left alone to be responsible for their actions.

In Skinner's view, the more investigation proceeds into the relationship between behaviour and its consequences, the more the findings 'take over the explanatory functions previously assigned to personalities, states of mind, feelings, traits of character, purposes and intentions'. Apparently, by the time Skinner had finished the book he claimed that he 'actually did not feel' that he had written it because 'the book was the inevitable consequence' of what had happened to him and what he had read (Schatzman, 1990).

Skinner's ideas have had a far-reaching impact and have occupied a powerful and central position in psychology. Skinner certainly promoted his ideas vigorously and throughout his lifetime argued persuasively against mentalistic analyses. Indeed, he is said to have been 'shaken' when one colleague, watching a squirrel running in a cage, suggested that the squirrel *liked* it, and 'dismayed' when another spoke of a roadside advertisement holding the *attention* too long.

Skinner has often been portrayed as being responsible for a demeaning and simplistic view of humans as 'biological machines', reacting to external events in their environment. Some psychologists do not agree. For them, Skinner should ultimately be seen as humane, pointing out how humans are controlled and advocating the acknowledgement of this to construct a more liberal society.

Talking points

1 B.F. Skinner is one of the best known of all psychologists and is arguably one of the most important contributors to the development of modern psychology. His death in 1990 triggered off a series of reviews and evaluations of his work which exposed a variety of misunderstandings, prejudices and long-standing controversies. The article was written by Stuart Sutherland, a critic of Skinner. According to Sutherland 'it is only too easy to demonstrate the inadequacy of Skinner's views about operant behaviour.'

Sutherland suggests that the repeated pairing of an electric shock with the sound of a buzzer results in the buzzer eventually coming to be feared. However, the fear, evinced as both behavioural responses and a subjective feeling, receives no reinforcement whatsoever. 'Indeed', suggests Sutherland, 'if anything, the response is punished'. Do you think Sutherland's example really does demonstrate the inadequacy of Skinner's views?

2 A further criticism made by Sutherland concerns the limited application that Skinner's behavioural methods have in the treatment of people with psychological problems. Although Sutherland accepts that some treatments are useful, he suggests that the more successful ones derive from Pavlov's research rather than Skinner's. Thus, classical conditioning is useful in the treatment of phobias, but operant conditioning techniques merely improve outward behaviour and do not make the person 'feel better'.

Sutherland also suggests that with Skinnerian approaches, improvements in behaviour are limited to the therapeutic setting in which the behavioural methods are used, and do not continue once the person has left the setting and reinforcements can no longer be given. Is Sutherland correct or is there evidence to suggest that approaches based on operant conditioning can **a)** explain the aetiology of psychological disorder and **b)** provide a basis for its effective treatment?

3 Sutherland notes that Skinner 'on occasion practised his methods on himself'. Skinner also applied his methods to his children. When his first daughter Debbie was old enough to be put on a toilet seat, Skinner attached a musical box to the seat. As soon as a few drops of moisture struck a strip of paper under the seat, the music box began to play *The Blue Danube*. Skinner suggested that 'the music was reinforcing', and his daughter quickly learned to urinate in order to make the music box play!

Despite the above 'success', Sutherland criticises Skinner for failing to apply the very conditioning processes he advocated to the treatment of his own acrophobia (fear of heights) and his wife's claustrophobia (fear of enclosed spaces). What do you think Skinner's response would have been to Sutherland's criticism? What other 'unusual' ways did Skinner believe operant conditioning techniques could be applied?

4 In *Beyond Freedom and Dignity*, Skinner (1971) advocated that his ideas and principles of learning should be adopted by society as a whole. Society normally allocates responsibility to individuals and punishes them when wrongdoings are committed. Skinner, however, argued that 'freedom' is a meaningless and illusory concept since behaviour is simply the result of genetic predispositions and past conditioning history (as Sutherland notes, 'to predict what a person would do next all one needs to know is the history of reinforcement to which he has been subjected'). Thus, Skinner argued that society should not worry about blaming people for their transgressions but should instead concentrate on future reinforcement contingencies.

Skinner's application of his ideas to society as a whole have perhaps been the most controversial. Critics such as Sutherland argue that Skinner's approach dehumanises people and leads to a rigid form of social control because it suggests that it is 'possible to control everybody's behaviour by applying rewards and punishments in the right way.' But which would you prefer: a society in which you are left alone but punished when you do wrong, or one in which good things happen to you for socially acceptable behaviour whilst irresponsible behaviour is subject to re-education rather than punishment?

5 Sutherland also criticises Skinner for over-simplifying and restricting behaviour. For example, he notes that 'there is not much an animal can do [when in a Skinner box] except press the bar.' For Sutherland 'it is here that Skinner's simple-minded theory breaks down … A rat taught to press a bar with its foot in order to gain food will sit on the bar if its feet are tied together … The attempt to explain behaviour without acknowledging internal factors was bound to fail.'

Skinner, however, felt that such simplification was essential. For him, 'a scientific analysis doesn't have a place for the individual as an initiator of behaviour.' Skinner believed that psychology had failed to make the same progress as the 'natural' sciences precisely because it had failed to implement their rigorous, focused approaches. Development in the natural sciences is characterised by the successive formulation of theories and specific tests of hypotheses derived from these. In order to be sure of what is going on, a researcher has to look at the effect of changing only one thing at a time. For example, the type of reinforcement used could be changed and the effects of this on the response of bar pressing be observed. If nothing else has been altered, any change in bar pressing must be due to the change in the type of reinforcement.

Do you agree with Sutherland's suggestion that Skinner's approach is an extreme simplification of the true complexity of behaviour? How do you think more meaningful investigations of rat behaviour could be carried out?

6 Blackman (1990) has pointed out that contrary to the public perception of him, Skinner did not work exclusively with rats and pigeons (as Sutherland seems to imply). Rather he attempted to analyse cognitive terms and the concept of 'consciousness' itself. Certain cognitive approaches see consciousness as a 'higher executive system'. Skinner and others would argue that this simply begs the question of what controls the higher executive system. Presumably this would be an even higher process controlled by another, and so on *ad infinitum*.

What approach to the concept of consciousness do you think Skinner would take? What do you think Skinner meant when he wrote at the end of the third volume of his autobiography (1983), 'If I am right about human behaviour I have written the autobiography of a non-person'?

7 Sutherland sees Skinner as being 'the last of the behaviourists or at least the last of any note' who 'promised more than he could fulfil'. Whilst acknowledging that some of Skinner's early work was important, Sutherland suggests that his status as a 'guru' in psychology severely held up progress in the discipline. Although it is true that Skinner resisted the increasing emphasis on cognitive approaches to behaviour, the development of psychology does not seem to have been adversely affected. Indeed, cognitive and behaviourist approaches are seen by some as being complementary rather than competitive. What is the interface between the two approaches called, and how can this interface account for forms of learning such as exploring a maze (Tolman, 1967) which occur without reinforcement or punishment?

8 One challenge to Skinner's ideas not mentioned by Sutherland is work which shows that some animals are particularly likely to learn certain specific behaviours. This can happen even when the consequences are widely separated from the behaviour. Perhaps the most famous example of this is an experiment reported by Garcia, Ervin and Koelling (1966). Rats were allowed to eat some new food and, much later, became ill (the illness was actually caused by the experimenters irradiating the rats). Simple conditioning theory would predict that the rats should only associate events close together in time. In fact, however, Garcia et al. reported that they very quickly learned to avoid the food.

Is there any way in which Skinner could account for Garcia et al.'s observation? Why do rats have this particular learning ability, and can you think of examples in which a similar effect is observed in humans?

References and further reading

Those references which are particularly worthy of further reading are indicated thus: *, together with a brief description of their area of concern.

*Blackman, D. (1990) 'Not a rat man but a people man', *The Guardian*, August 24th. *This is Blackman's spirited reply to Sutherland's obituary of Skinner.*

*Ferster, C. & Skinner, B.F. (1957) *Schedules of Reinforcement*, New York: Appleton-Century-Crofts. *In this book Ferster and Skinner provide a detailed account of the effects of various schedules (fixed/variable, ratio/interval) on behaviour.*

Garcia, J., Ervin, F. & Koelling, R. (1966) 'Learning with prolonged delay of reinforcement', *Psychonomic Science*, 4, pp. 123–4.

Pavlov, I.P. (1927) *Conditioned Reflexes*, London: Oxford University Press.

Schatzman, M. (1990) 'Obituaries: B.F. Skinner', *The Independent*, August 21st.

Skinner, B.F. (1938) *The Behaviour of Organisms*, New York: Appleton-Century-Crofts.

*Skinner, B.F. (1948) *Walden Two*, New York: Macmillan. *Skinner's classic fictional outline of a modern Utopia. Set in the United States, it portrays a society in which human problems are solved by a scientific technology of human conduct.*

Skinner, B.F. (1957) *Verbal Behaviour*, New York: Appleton-Century-Crofts.

Skinner, B.F. (1968) *The Technology of Teaching*, New York: Appleton-Century-Crofts.

*Skinner, B.F. (1971) *Beyond Freedom and Dignity*, London: Jonathon Cape. *This book caused enormous controversy when it was published. In America it was attacked by right-wing politicians as a 'serious threat to liberty', and was the subject of a Congressional investigation.*

*Skinner, B.F. (1983) *A Matter of Consequence*, New York: Appleton-Century-Crofts. *This is the third volume of Skinner's autobiography, the other two being 'Particulars of My Life' (1976) and 'The Shaping of a Behaviourist' (1978).*

Tolman, E.C. (1967) *Purposive Behaviour in Animals and Men*, New York: Irvington.

Watson, J.B. (1930) *Behaviourism*, New York: Norton.

6

SWITCH IN THE SHOCK TACTICS

Switch in the shock tactics

© *The Guardian*

Of all the questionable things that psychiatrists do to patients, electroshock, or electroconvulsive therapy (ECT), raises more questions – and hackles – than most. It's easy to understand why. For many people, the public image of ECT comes straight out of *One Flew Over the Cuckoo's Nest*.

Someone is held down and has electrodes applied to his head. He goes into spasms. It looks frightful and seems to have similarities to torture techniques. Psychiatry may be a slightly mysterious branch of medicine and psychiatrists are often given more benefit of the doubt than we probably deserve, but to the man – and potential patient – in the street it must seem pretty obvious that plugging people into the mains, which is what it seems like, is harmful. Most people have experienced accidental electric shocks and know that electricity can be lethal. Surely it fries their brains?

ECT is used mainly in severe depression unresponsive to other approaches and is generally given as a single course of six or eight treatments at the rate of two or three a week. Even these short courses are too much for anti-ECT activists to accept. In some American states ECT

has practically been outlawed. Some psychiatrists also feel a bit uneasy about ECT, as one might expect from the slightly wimpish, permissive image psychiatrists have among more robust medics. (There is some truth in the claim that a psychiatrist is a doctor who can't stand the sight of blood.)

Well, let the sceptics ponder a recent report in the *British Journal of Psychiatry* describing the beneficial effects in a 67-year-old woman who had had ECT every two weeks for over 18 months because it was the only treatment that helped her.

Four previous episodes of severe depression during the previous 28 years had responded to ECT but the symptoms – which included delusions and hallucinations – kept recurring. Antidepressant drugs were ineffective. She agreed to try one ECT treatment every fortnight in the hope of preventing the regular relapses. It worked well.

Having been an in-patient for most of the previous two years, she was discharged after a few months and had subsequent ECTs as an out-patient. She was now 70 and lived in a nursing home, but was evidently managing well, and was sufficiently in touch with current affairs to have organised a knitting club to help a Romanian orphanage. Psychological tests of brain function showed that, far from having been 'fried', her brain was working well. Most importantly, she had not been clinically depressed or suicidal.

ECT can affect the memory although the effects are usually restricted to the period of treatment. Tests showed that this patient's memory had not been impaired after a year of fortnightly ECT except for events on the day of the treatment. The authors note a previous report of a post mortem examination on an elderly woman who had undergone 1250

ECTs in 26 years. No evidence of brain damage attributable to treatment (as opposed to ageing) was found. They point out that modern ECT machines are probably an improvement on cruder predecessors.

Before ECT, convulsions – thought to be the therapeutic component of the treatment – were induced by drugs. These took up to an hour to produce a fit and the build-up period was usually very distressing. Producing fits by electricity – originally without anaesthesia – was intended as a humane alternative. It may sound barbaric but, because an epileptic convulsion causes amnesia for events shortly before the fit, the actual electric shock is never remembered. Anaesthesia is used not to prevent the discomfort of the shock but because muscle relaxants are now routinely used to reduce the risk of injury during convulsions. Being conscious but paralysed is a horrible experience, so an anaesthetic is given before the relaxant. ECT is no more 'barbaric' than any other procedure done under general anaesthesia.

There is a large placebo or 'magical' element in ECT and I have seen patients improve dramatically after sham ECT involving anaethesia but no actual shock. ECT was introduced in 1938 well before the age of routine controlled clinical trials, but in the past 15 years several trials have compared real and sham ECT. It is now clear that significantly more respond to the real thing.

It was undoubtedly overused at one time but it remains a valuable technique despite advances in the pharmacological and psychological treatment of depression. It also has some advantages over antidepressant drugs since the side effects of ECT usually wear off quickly, whereas those of anti-depressants may last as long as the course of treatment and it is impossible for patients to take an accidental or deliberate overdose of ECT.

Since several hundred people die every year from suicidal anti-depressant overdoses, that is not a trivial point. ECT saves quite a few lives.

Background

The idea that the inducement of a shock to the body can have a beneficial therapeutic effect in the treatment of mental disorders is not new. As early as 1933, Sakel (reported in Fink, 1984) reported that insulin-induced hypoglycaemic comas brought about a noticeable improvement in the behaviour of psychotic individuals. For some reason, it seemed that the sudden drop in blood sugar and the coincident convulsions produced by excessive insulin decreased the episodes of thought disturbance amongst that group of individuals.

A few years later a Hungarian physician, von Meduna, observed that schizophrenia rarely occurred in people with epilepsy (and vice versa), and that psychotic patients who were prone to epilepsy showed less severe symptoms after each seizure. On the basis of these observations which, as it later transpired, were only partially correct, von Meduna concluded that schizophrenia and epilepsy were incompatible or 'biologically antagonistic'. Drawing on Sakel's work, von Meduna reasoned that by inducing a major epileptiform fit, which could be achieved by means of an intravenous injection of a cerebral stimulant called cardiazol, the schizophrenia would be 'driven out' and the schizophrenic 'cured'.

Whilst von Meduna's results appeared to show some sort of treatment effect, cardiazol was a somewhat unsatisfactory method of inducing a fit since, amongst other things, the drug gave rise to feelings of impending death during the conscious phase of its action! Various other methods of inducing a fit were tried until, after visiting an abattoir and seeing animals rendered unconscious through the use of an electric shock, Ugo Cerletti and Lucio Bini (Bini, 1938) advocated passing an electric current across the temples to induce the epileptic fit.

Although there have been refinements to Cerletti and Bini's technique, electroconvulsive therapy (or ECT, electroplexy, or electroshock) is administered in essentially the way developed by them. Prior to the treatment, the individual is given a full physical examination (since heart conditions, chest diseases, and peptic ulcers can be accentuated by ECT). The patient is also required to fast for a period of three to four hours prior to the treatment and is requested to empty his/her bladder immediately before the treatment. In its early days, ECT was given 'straight', that is, without anaesthetic. 'Modified' ECT is now the norm and short-acting anaesthetics (such as sodium thiopentone or methohexitol) are used, for reasons which are described below.

As the individual is being psychologically prepared for the treatment (something which is necessary given the negative public image the therapy has), dentures, rings, and other metallic objects are removed and the person is dressed in a loose fitting gown. About 45–60 minutes before the treatment, an injection of 0.6–0.8 milligrams of atropine sulphate is given. This drug prevents the possibility of disturbances to the heart's normal rhythm and inhibits the secretion of mucus in the lungs, and of saliva, which the anaesthetised person cannot cough up. A person who is particularly anxious and apprehensive may be given valium (10 milligrams) or sodium amytal (120–200 milligrams). Relaxation can also be achieved by continuous soothing music played during the therapy session.

With the person lying on his/her back, head supported by a pillow, an intravenous injection of a short-acting anaesthetic is given. This is followed by an injection of a muscle relaxant such as scoline (suxamethonium chloride). The person is given oxygen before and after the application of the electric current, and a mouth gag is placed between the teeth to prevent biting of the tongue or lips during the fit.

Saline-soaked lint covered electrodes are then attached to each temple (termed 'bilateral ECT') or two electrodes are placed over the temple and mastoid region of whichever cerebral hemisphere has been ascertained to be non-dominant (termed 'unilateral ECT'). With the chin held still, an electric current of around 200 milliamps flowing at 110 volts is passed from one electrode to the other for a period of about 1½ seconds (although there are individual differences in terms of both the quantity and duration of the current depending on the type and method of ECT treatment applied).

If an anaesthetic has not been used, an immediate loss of consciousness occurs. If a muscle relaxant has not been used, a convulsion similar to a grand mal epileptic seizure occurs. This consists of a rapid contraction and relaxation of the muscles which lasts for about a minute. It is the firing of the neurons that control movement which produces the convulsions – muscular rigidity and trembling followed by movement of the head, trunk and limbs. In the early days of ECT's use, the initial seizure often produced convulsions that were so violent the dorsal vertebrae were fractured (sometimes through the convulsion itself and sometimes through what might be described as 'over-zealous nursing restraint').

With muscle relaxants, however, the person may need to be gently restrained, but the convulsions are not seen. Indeed, the only observable signs of the convulsion are a slight twitching of the eyelids, facial muscles and toes. Thus, muscle relaxants reduce the convulsions but not the seizure, and therefore it is the seizure (rather than anything else) which must produce the therapeutic effects. When the convulsion is complete and when the jaw is relaxed, an airway is inserted into the mouth and the person is oxygenated until she/he resumes breathing unaided. The person is then turned into the left lateral position, head on the side, and is carefully observed until the effects of the muscle relaxant and anaesthetic have worn off, and the person has recovered completely.

Therapy typically involves a number of treatments occurring over a period of several weeks. The total number of treatments is gauged by the individual's response. In some cases improvement occurs rapidly, sometimes within half a dozen treatments. In other cases, double this number of treatments may be required before any improvement is observed. In the event of a recurrence of the disorder which necessitated the ECT, further treatments are required otherwise the person does not derive as much benefit as she/he otherwise would.

Early studies of ECT's effectiveness revealed that it did sometimes produce dramatic improvements, although not in schizophrenics, the very condition the method was originally devised to treat. It seemed that those who benefited most from ECT were depressives who had been misdiagnosed as schizophrenic (Hays, 1971). Today, ECT is primarily used in cases of severe depression, particularly the endogenous type which have failed to respond to other forms of treatment. It is also sometimes used in the treatment of manic-depression, certain obsessive–compulsive disorders and (perhaps surprisingly given what has been said above), catatonic schizophrenia during the stuporous phase. Although it is not completely understood why ECT is effective, the evidence overwhelmingly supports its effectiveness in providing significant relief from depression in a proportion of individuals (Frankel, 1984).

Talking points

1 According to the article, part of ECT's negative public image derives from horrific descriptions of the treatment in films and books. Indeed, it has been argued that the common impression is that ECT 'is about as scientific as kicking a television set because it is not working' (Heather, 1976). Yet whilst the treatment is painless (due to the use of an anaesthetic) and although ECT is now considered to be a low risk therapeutic procedure, the public image it has makes many referred for the therapy extremely frightened.

Suppose you were made responsible for devising a campaign to promote ECT as a therapy. Using the article and the **Background** information, what positive aspects would you highlight in order to change the public's perception of ECT? Now consider a campaign that was designed to achieve the opposite. What negative aspects of ECT would you wish to highlight? According to Sackheim (1985), ECT is still used on some 60 000–100 000 people per year in the USA, and in England alone the figure is nearer to 100 000. Given the pros and cons you have identified for ECT, what in your view most influences the 'cost-benefit' analysis of the therapy?

2 The article also describes the case of a 67-year-old woman who evidently benefited from a course of ECT treatment, which was administered after other treatments had failed to produce any noticeable improvement. Several reviews of the relevant therapeutic literature (e.g. Scovern & Kilmann, 1980) have found ECT to be 'highly effective', particularly with endogenously depressed and suicidal individuals. On the other hand some writers (e.g. Costello, 1976) have criticised studies of ECT's effectiveness for using poor methodology, such as failing to employ objective appraisals of treatment efficacy and control groups.

Why do you think that ECT might be particularly useful for suicidal individuals, and how could its effectiveness within that population be assessed? How else do you think the general effectiveness of ECT could be assessed apart from using the criteria mentioned in **1** above? What do you think Costello (1976) means in his critique of ECT's effectiveness when he talks of studies 'failing to employ objective appraisals', and how could this particular problem be overcome?

3 If ECT is as effective as its proponents claims, why do you think the American Psychiatric Association (1978) recommended that it should only be used as a treatment of 'last resort', which should only be attempted when drugs have not worked or cannot be used for medical reasons? Although the appropriate use of ECT should be preceded by a careful assessment of the costs and benefits for a given individual, Breggin (1979), in a devastating review of the potentially damaging effects of ECT, pointed out that such assessments are not necessarily routine. What sorts of issues concerning the rights of patients do you think might arise in this connection?

4 Many theories, both biological and psychological, have been proposed to explain how ECT works, although none is clearly supported by research evidence. ECT is sometimes associated with memory loss and it has been suggested that amnesia can account for its effectiveness. It is true that following ECT the person remembers nothing about the shock or convulsion (the regaining of consciousness is usually associated with confusion and disorientation).

Both anterograde amnesia (the inability to store new memories) and retrograde amnesia (the inability to retrieve memories prior to the treatment) have been documented. Although anterograde amnesia gradually disappears after the therapy, at least one study (Squire & Slater, 1983) has indicated that retrograde amnesia can last for years. How could you investigate the suggestion that memory loss accounts for the effectiveness of ECT, and do you think that the evidence presented in the article offer any support for the 'memory loss' theory?

5 One early explanation for the effectiveness of von Meduna's use of cerebral stimulants was that the effects were so terrifying even the most disturbed individual would deny his/her symptoms in order to avoid the treatment. Another theory of ECT's effectiveness argues that, given the nature of the therapy, the person denies his/her symptoms in order to avoid the 'punishment' the ECT comes to be perceived as, and this extinguishes the abnormal behaviour. How do you think this proposal could be assessed experimentally?

A third theoretical approach suggests that ECT works by producing a variety of biochemical changes in the brain and that these changes are much greater than those produced by other forms of somatic therapy (i.e. drugs). Given that ECT seems to be most effective in treating endogenous depression, what sorts of biochemical substances might possibly be involved, if indeed such changes do occur? If ECT does influence neural transmission within the brain, what brain structures would you suggest might be influenced by the therapy?

6 Kupfer (1976) and Vogel, Vogel, McAbee and Thurmond (1980) have reported that depressed individuals **a)** enter rapid-eye movement sleep sooner than normal people, and **b)** spend a longer time in this state during the last half of sleep. How could you use these findings to explain ECT's effectiveness, and what additional evidence concerning the biochemical action of antidepressant drugs could be used to offer support for your explanation?

7 In view of the lack of knowledge about exactly how ECT works, the therapy has, as noted in the article, 'practically been outlawed'. Indeed, in 1982 in Berkeley, California, the therapy *was* outlawed by voter referendum and the administration of ECT was made a misdemeanour punishable by a fine of up to $500 and six months in jail. Although the ban was later reversed by the courts, the strength of opposition to ECT was clearly demonstrated by the fact that voters passed the ban. What is your view on this obviously ethical issue? Should any form of therapy be used in the absence of a widely accepted explanation for its effectiveness especially when, as claimed by Breggin (1979), there is evidence to show that brain damage can occur following the administration of ECT?

8 According to the article, 'there is a large "magical" element in ECT'. This has been shown in 'sham' ECT studies (e.g. Fink, 1979) in which all the procedures except the electric shock are undertaken. How could you use 'sham' ECT procedures to devise an investigation to examine the effects of therapist and patient 'expectations' of ECT's effectiveness? There are several variations on 'standard' ECT. Try and find out what is involved in the following **a** electronarcosis, **b** the Glissando technique, and **c** the Ectronous technique. Do these techniques raise any ethical issues?

References and further reading

Those references which are particularly worthy of further reading are indicated thus: *, together with a brief description of their area of concern.

American Psychiatric Association (1978) *Electroconvulsive Therapy*, Washington, D.C.: Author.

Bini, L. (1938) 'Experimental researches on epileptic attacks induced by the electric current', *American Journal of Psychiatry*, Supplement 94, pp. 172–83.

Breggin, P.R. (1979) *Electroshock: Its Brain Disabling Effects*, New York: Springer Verlag.

*Costello, C.G. (1976) 'Electroconvulsive therapy: is further investigation necessary?' *Canadian Psychiatric Association Journal*, 21, pp. 61–7. *A critical account of ECT which has been attacked for being 'polemical', but which nonetheless offers interesting arguments against the use of ECT.*

*Fink, M. (1979) *Convulsive Therapy: Theory and Practice*, New York: Raven Press. *Possibly the definitive account of the nature and application of ECT.*

*Fink, M. (1984) 'Meduna and the origins of convulsive therapy in suicidal patients', *American Journal of Psychiatry*, 141, pp. 1034–41. *An interesting historical account of the early uses of ECT.*

Frankel, F.H. (1984) 'The use of electroconvulsive therapy in suicidal patients', *American Journal of Psychotherapy*, 38, pp. 384–91.

*Hays, P. (1971) *New Horizons in Psychiatry*, Harmondsworth: Penguin. *Although somewhat dated, this offers an excellent account of the controversies surrounding the use of ECT.*

Heather, N. (1976) *Radical Perspectives in Psychology*, London: Methuen.

Kupfer, D.J. (1976) 'REM latency: A psychobiologic marker for primary depressive disease', *Biological Psychiatry*, 11, pp. 159–74.

*Sackheim, H.A. (1985) 'The case for ECT', *Psychology Today*, 19(6), pp. 36–40. *A thorough and very readable account of the arguments for ECT as a therapeutic agent.*

*Scovern, A.W. & Kilmann, P.R. (1980) 'Status of electroconvulsive therapy: a review of the outcome literature', *Psychological Bulletin*, 87, pp. 260–303. *A comprehensive literature review of ECT's effectiveness.*

Squire, L.R. & Slater, P.C. (1983) 'Electroconvulsive therapy and complaints of memory dysfunction: a prospective three year follow-up study', *British Journal of Psychiatry*, 142, pp. 1–8.

Vogel, G.W., Vogel, F., McAbee, R.S. & Thurmond, A.G. (1980) 'Improvement of depression by REM sleep deprivation', *Archives of General Psychiatry*, 37, pp. 247–53.

7

A ROSE BY ANY OTHER NAME

A rose by any other name

Deborah Holder
© *The Guardian*

What's in a name? Well, if you're set on a career as the screen's leading tough guy and your name is Marion, quite a lot. It's hardly surprising he opted for John (Wayne) instead. Likewise for Marilyn Monroe, once plain old Norma Jean. That had to go, along with the mousy hair and extra pounds, to make way for blonde curls and a name better suited to fame.

More often, however, the equation operates the other way round: rather than the image determining the name, recent studies suggest the name can determine the image. Sussex University researchers Helen Petrie and Carol Lee Johnson asked 255 students to rate a list of 86 names in terms of masculinity or femininity, and then to complete a questionnaire to reveal how typically they, as individuals, fitted male or female stereotypes. The five most feminine names emerged as Sophie, Elizabeth, Emily, Lucy and Rose. Petrie and Johnson found women with these and other 'feminine' names had more 'feminine' personalities.

They suggest two possible explanations for this: it may be that parents who choose a more feminine name are more likely to encourage feminine behaviour. David, father of two-year-old Sophie and four-year-old Matt, for example, acknowledges that from the moment his daughter was born, he thought of her as 'a very female creature'. He liked the name specifically because it sounded feminine and matched his image of her as a 'fragile little girl'. It would seem logical that fluffy toys and frilly frocks will follow, and a self-fulfilling prophecy will be set in motion.

The second influence on the Sophies and the Lucys is likely to come from not-so-significant others and the way in which they respond to a name. While those who know a child's parents and family background should be less vulnerable to name-based stereotyping, others, with little else to go on, may use it as a cue when forming a first impression.

Although based on factors as apparently superficial as clothes, hair colour and weight, first impressions are not to be underestimated. The responses of others are not only important in their gradual, long-term effect on self-image; they can also have more direct consequences. For instance, a doctor who finds that she has a Lucinda Wallis-Smythe and a Darren Watts on her list may form a different mental picture of each before even meeting them. The questions she asks and the treatment she recommends may differ accordingly.

This might sound like advanced paranoia, but teachers have been found guilty of precisely this type of stereotyping. American psychologists McDavid and Harari found that teachers gave significantly higher marks to essays bearing 'desirable' names. 'David', for instance, was consistently perceived as good, strong, wise, serious and masculine, whereas 'Harold' was seen as weak, foolish, humorous, simple and unsociable. In general, unusual names were seen less favourably

'I remember people often saying, "What a pretty name" and "Your name really suits you",' says Samantha, now 30. She has only recently started calling herself Sam. 'I never liked it when I was younger but now I find I am using it myself, mostly on the phone at work.'

Her change of heart coincided with a promotion and Sam concedes she may have rejected the softer, less threatening Samantha in favour of a friendly but firm alternative more appropriate to her new position.

Helen Petrie's research confirms that many more women than men use diminutives. These are almost always androgynous or masculine and may be a means of rejecting the feminine name and stereotype foisted on them at birth. 'I remember wanting both options,' says June. 'At around 12, I desperately wanted to be called Georgina or Josephine, so I could shorten my name to fit the tomboy image I had of myself but also have an elegant, feminine name in reserve. I was consciously rejecting a "girlie" name but at the same time I wanted to play it safe.'

A reminder that we actually set more store by names than we care to acknowledge can come with the responsibility of naming another. Suzanna remembers the naming process as harrowing. 'Legally you have 42 days to name your child and only the fear of a fine got us down there on the last day. I hadn't expected it to be such an issue but it seemed vital to choose a name exactly right for her. I began to think about the reaction she might get if I stuck her with an unusual name. In the back of my mind I knew a name would have social repercussions.'

So what if Marilyn had stuck to her original name? We might think of 'Norma' rather differently now: instead of its frumpy associations it would be synonymous with glamour, femininity and sex. Speculating on the implications is fascinating – what, one wonders, would Norma Major's image be?

Background

In a very early study on the processes involved in interpersonal perception, Asch (1946) showed that when people are presented with characteristics describing a person, they tend to go beyond the information presented and assume that the person also possesses certain other characteristics. For example, Asch found that when people were presented with a list containing the words 'intelligent', 'skilful', 'industrious', 'warm', 'determined', 'practical' and 'cautious', it was also inferred that the person was 'serious' rather than 'frivolous', 'persistent' rather than 'unstable', and so on. Asch also showed that certain words had much more impact on the inferences that were made than others. Thus, 'warm' and 'cold' had a greater effect than 'polite' and 'blunt'. Asch used the term 'central trait' to describe words which had an impact and 'peripheral trait' to describe those which played a less influential role.

According to Bruner and Tagiuri (1954) our perceptions of others is not based on what those others are 'really' like, but on our own general 'theory' or expectations about them. Put another way, everyone has an idea of which personality traits go with, or are consistent with, other personality traits and this is used to 'fill in the gaps' in our representations of particular people. Bruner and Tagiuri coined the term 'implicit personality theory' to describe the unconscious inference processes which enable us to form impressions of others on the basis of very little evidence.

Bruner and Tagiuri suggest that implicit personality theories are shared by everyone and are consistent within a given culture. This explains, for example, why many people think that bulging eyes are a sign of extroversion, that intellectuals have larger than average skulls, and that thick lips mean gluttony (Leyens & Codol, 1988). Indeed, so entrenched are such beliefs, despite evidence to the contrary, that the term 'illusory correlation' has been used to describe them (Chapman & Chapman, 1969).

Although our implicit theory of personality is at least partly derived from our background culture, individual experiences of interacting with and making judgements about people also provides us with a set of assumptions and inferences. These may not be shared with other people. For example, one student in a class who hears that a new member is 'vivacious' might feel differently from another student, depending on their previous experiences. Moreover, since certain languages such as Eskimo and Maori embody very different theories about people to those embodied in the English language (Harré, 1983), their perception of others is likely to be very different to our own since they begin with a very different set of basic categorisations (Abrahams & Stanley, 1992). As Abrahams and Stanley note, we share a basic theory of others through our language, but we develop personal variations through our particular social experience.

'Implicit personality theory' has been demonstrated through a number of different experimental techniques and has been shown to manifest itself in a number of different ways (Gahagan, 1980). One of these is the phenomenon of stereotyping. The concept of a 'stereotype' was introduced to psychology by Walter Lippman (1922). The word derives from its use in printing, where it refers to a solid printing mould or plate which, once cast, is difficult to change (Reber, 1985).

In implicit personality theory, a single item of information about a person will generate inferences about other aspects of that person's character. In stereotyping, information is limited to some highly visible aspect of a person, such as his/her race, sex, nationality and so on. This information generates judgements about what any person belonging to a given group is like (an 'individual' stereotype) and that all people belonging to a given group possess the same characteristics (a 'group' stereotype). Social stereotypes can thus be defined as grossly oversimplified and overgeneralised abstractions that people share about their own group or about another group.

Early research examined the ways in which different ethnic groups were stereotyped. For example, Katz and Braly (1933) asked Princeton University students to indicate which five of a list of one hundred words describing personality were most closely associated with each of 84 ethnic groups (such as Germans, Negroes, and Jews). Katz and Braly used agreement across students as the criterion for the existence of a stereotype. Thus, if 75 per cent or more of students assigned the trait of, say, 'obedience' to a given ethnic group, that was taken as evidence of the existence of a stereotype.

The results showed a high degree of agreement amongst the students. For example, 84 per cent thought Negroes were 'superstitious', 79 per cent thought Jews were 'shrewd', and 78 per cent thought Germans were 'scientifically minded'. The results were also used to compare different ethnic groups in terms of their favourability. In 1933, Americans had the best stereotype and Turks the worst. By using the same method as Katz and Braly, other researchers have been able to examine the ways in which stereotypes change over time.

For example, Gilbert's (1951) study of Princeton students showed that the three stereotypes described earlier and reported by Katz and Braly had become significantly weaker. Thus, only 41 per cent thought Negroes were 'superstitious', 47 per cent thought Jews were 'shrewd' and 62 per cent thought Germans were 'scientifically minded'. Later research (e.g. Karlins, Coffman & Walters, 1969) showed that whilst Americans were seen as industrious, intelligent but not especially materialistic in 1933, by 1967 they were seen as materialistic but not especially industrious or intelligent. Such research also revealed changes in the favourability of ethnic groups. By 1969, for example, Turks had improved quite markedly in terms of their favourability whilst Americans had lost their position slightly.

As interesting as such findings are, one of the criticisms that has been made of research in this area is that it forces judgements and is subject to the artefacts of social desirability responding (Gahagan, 1991). In 1969, Princeton students were markedly less willing to engage in the exercise than was the case previously. Since negative stereotypes have become less acceptable, people would be less likely to offer a negative stereotype even if such a stereotype was in fact held by them.

One way of overcoming the possibility of social desirability responding was devised by Razran over 40 years ago (Razran, 1950). Participants in his study were led to believe they would be rating pictures of girls according to various psychological qualities. At a later time, the participants were shown the same pictures but this time each girl was identified with an Irish, Italian or Jewish-sounding name. Razran used changes in the ratings previously given as evidence of ethnic stereotyping. Amongst other things, Razran reported that girls with Jewish sounding names were rated higher in terms of 'intelligence' and 'ambition' but lower on 'niceness'. Razran argued that since the participants in his study did not know they were involved in a study on stereotyping, their responses were free of social desirability responding.

Talking points

1 One question of central importance in this area of research is where our stereotypes about others come from. According to Campbell (1967), stereotypes originate from two major sources – a person's experiences with a particular person or group of people and the communication of those experiences to others. For example, if the stereotypical view of Scots is that they are extremely thrifty, someone at some time must have encountered an extremely thrifty Scot. Equally, if Germans are stereotyped as 'getting up at dawn to reserve a sunbed', someone at some time must have observed this.

At one time, then, the stereotypical characteristic attributed to a given group must have been an attribute of at least one member of that group. Later on, the process of communication would establish the stereotype as a truism in the minds of many people. Stereotypes therefore originate in someone's experience and consequently must contain at least a 'grain of truth' (Wegner & Vallacher, 1976). How do you think the 'grain of truth' hypothesis could be applied to male and female name stereotyping, and how could empirical evidence for the hypothesis be gathered?

2 One criticism of the 'grain of truth' hypothesis is that it assumes that a person, who was at one time in a particular situation, made a perfectly logical inference, that is, the person's expectancies and inferences reflected his/her experiences exactly. As noted in the **Background**, however, people sometimes see two variables as being related when in fact they are not, a phenomenon known as 'illusory correlation'.

In connection with stereotypes, people perceive differences between two or more social groups in terms of the strength of correlation between membership in one of the groups and certain characteristics even when such differences do not exist (Baron, 1989). For example, Sanbonmatsu, Shavitt, Sherman and Rosko-Edoldsen (1987) showed that participants in their study held the view that people of Cuban descent were more violent than people of European descent even though being Cuban or European is equally unrelated to this characteristic. Can you think of a way in which the phenomenon of illusory correlation can be explained, and what sorts of consequences could illusory correlations have?

3 The research conducted by Petrie and Johnson suggests that women with 'feminine' names have more 'feminine' personalities. As the article suggests, one explanation for this may be that parents who chose 'feminine' names behave in a way which is more likely to encourage 'feminine' behaviour. Clearly, the stereotypes we hold of people can influence the ways in which we behave towards them. This may influence their behaviour in such a way that it confirms our stereotypical beliefs. Stereotypes may therefore be both self-fulfilling and self-perpetuating.

For example, a person with red hair may be perceived as possessing a fiery temper. This may lead other people to behave in ways which avoid making the person angry. This may in turn influence the person's behaviour: if a person is expected to exhibit a fiery temper she/he may do so even in response to mild provocation. This, then, merely confirms the view that red heads have a fiery temper! There is evidence to suggest that self-fulfilling prophecies do occur with respect to a range of stereotypes including those based on race, religion and sex (Christensen & Rosenthal, 1982). How could you test the hypothesis that forename stereotyping can lead to self-fulfilling behaviour?

4 Names are a central part of a person's self-concept and, as the article suggests, may form the basis for stereotyping and lead to the expectation of certain behaviours from a person with a given name. The Harari and McDavid (1973) study described in the article illustrated that essays allegedly written by children with names stereotyped by teachers as favourable and attractive (David, Michael, Karen and Lisa) received a full grade higher than names stereotyped as unfavourable and unattractive (Elmer, Hubert, Bertha and Adele). What role does the media play in at least partly creating stereotypical characteristics? Why do you think that 'John', once the most popular boys name, slipped to 40th place in the 1993 *Guinness Book of Names*?

5 The impression we form of others may be distorted because we focus on one particular characteristic that we expecially like or dislike and let it bias our perception of other aspects of the individual. The tendency to bias our judgements on the basis of one particular feature is known as the 'halo effect', and the bias may be positive or negative. As the article suggests, 'those who know a child's parents and family background should be less vulnerable to name stereotyping [while] others, with little else to go on, may use it as a cue when forming a first impression.' How could you test this hypothesis, and how could data supporting the hypothesis be explained?

6 According to the article, 'a doctor who finds that she has a Lucinda Wallis-Smythe and a Darren Watts on her list may form a different mental picture of each before ever meeting them. The questions she asks and treatment she recommends may differ accordingly.' A similar argument may be applied to the legal system, even though it is principle of law that a defendant should be tried on the basis of evidence rather than personal characteristics or background. However, no judge or jury can fail to notice aspects of a defendant's characteristics, and this might even include his or her name! What factors other than the available evidence might bias the views of a judge or jury? Are there any psychological research findings to support the claim that non-evidential factors actually do distort legal judgements?

7 In connection with the above, it has been noted that another feature of stereotyping is that it can influence how behaviour is interpreted and classified which can then influence how behaviour is recalled. Put another way, stereotyping can determine what is noticed in the first place and hence what is subsequently remembered (Gross, 1992). That humans do exhibit distortions in memory to fit current 'knowledge' was shown in a study conducted by Snyder and Uranowitz (1978).

Participants were given short biographies of 'Betty K.' from her birth to early adulthood. The biography included facts about her social life such as: 'Although she never had a steady boyfriend in school, she did go out on dates.' A week later, participants were given additional information about 'Betty K.'. Some were told that she later adopted a homosexual lifestyle whilst others were told that she later married (and adopted a heterosexual lifestyle). Later, participants were asked to recall 'Betty K's' original biography. The results showed that those participants told about her homosexual lifestyle were more likely to remember that 'she never had a steady boyfriend' than that 'she did go out on dates'. For participants told about her heterosexual lifestyle, the reverse findings were obtained.

These results suggest that people **a)** reconstruct memories of previous events to make them fit in with their stereotypes or **b)** use stereotypes to answer questions when original memories cannot be recalled (Bellezza & Bower, 1981). Suppose a court case hinges on the accuracy of eye-witness testimony. How could you convince a judge that such testimony is not always accurate? In what other real-life situations can the processes described above be seen at work?

References and further reading

Those references which are particularly worthy of further consideration are indicated thus: *, together with a brief description of their area of concern.

Abrahams, C. & Stanley, E. (1992) *Social Psychology for Nurses*, London: Edward Arnold.

Asch, S. (1946) 'Forming impressions of personality', *Journal of Abnormal and Social Psychology*, 41, pp. 258–90.

Baron, R.A. (1989) *Psychology: The Essential Science*, London: Allyn & Bacon.

*Bruner, J.S. & Tagiuri, R. (1954) 'The perception of people', **in** G. Lindzey (Ed.) *Handbook of Social Psychology* (Vol. II), Reading, MA: Addison-Wesley. *Bruner and Tagiuri's chapter summarises their classic work in person perception.*

Bellezza, F.S. & Bower, G.H. (1981) 'Person stereotypes and memory for people', *Journal of Personality and Social Psychology*, 41, pp. 856–65.

Christensen, D. & Rosenthal, R. (1982) 'Gender and nonverbal decoding skill as determinants of interpersonal expectancy effects', *Journal of Personality and Social Psychology*, 42, pp. 75–87.

Campbell, D.T. (1967) 'Stereotypes and the perception of group differences', *American Psychologist*, 22, pp. 817–29.

Chapman, L.J. & Chapman, J.P. (1969) 'Illusory correlation as an obstacle to the use of valid psychodiagnostic signs', *Journal of Abnormal Psychology*, 74, pp. 271–80.

Gahagan, J. (1980) 'Social interaction', **in** J. Radford & E. Govier (Eds.) *A Textbook of Psychology* (1st ed.), London: Sheldon Books.

*Gahagan, J. (1991) 'Understanding other people; understanding self', **in** J. Radford & E. Govier (Eds.) *A Textbook of Psychology* (2nd ed.). London: Routledge. *Gahagan provides an excellent introduction to the theory and research in the area of social stereotyping.*

Gilbert, G.M. (1951) 'Stereotype persistence and change among college students', *Journal of Abnormal and Social Psychology*, 46, pp. 245–54.

Gross, R.D. (1992) *Psychology: The Science of Mind and Behaviour*, London: Hodder & Stoughton.

Harari, H. & McDavid, J.W. (1973) 'Teachers' expectations and name stereotypes', *Journal of Educational Psychology*, 65, pp. 222-5.

Harré, R. (1983) *Personal Being*, Oxford: Blackwell.

Karlins, M., Coffman, T.L. & Walters, G. (1969) 'On the fading of social stereotypes: studies in three generations of college students', *Journal of Personality and Social Psychology*, 13, pp. 1–16.

Katz, D. & Braly, K.W. (1933) 'Racial stereotypes of one hundred college students', *Journal of Abnormal and Social Psychology*, 28, pp. 280–90.

*Leyons, J-P., & Codol, J-P. (1988) 'Social cognition', **in** M. Hewstone, W. Stroebe, J-P. Codol & G.M. Stephenson (Eds.) *Introduction to Social Psychology*, Oxford: Blackwell. *This chapter summarises most of the relevant theory and research in social cognition.*

Lippman, W. (1922) *Public Opinion*, New York: Harcourt.

*Razran, G. (1950) 'Ethnic dislikes and stereotypes: A laboratory study', *Journal of Abnormal and Social Psychology*, 45, pp. 7–27. *Razran's research is interesting for the methodology it uses to overcome the possibility of social desirability responding in the area of person perception research.*

Reber, A.S. (1985) *The Penguin Dictionary of Psychology*, Harmondsworth: Penguin.

Sanbonmatsu, D.M., Shavitt, S., Sherman, S.J. & Rosko-Ewoldsen, D.R. (1987) 'Illusory correlation in the perception of performance by self or a salient other', *Journal of Experimental Social Psychology*, 23, pp. 518–43.

Snyder, M. & Uranowitz, S.W. (1978) 'Reconstructing the past: some cognitive consequences of person perception', *Journal of Personality and Social Psychology*, 36, pp. 941–50.

*Wegner, D.M. & Vallacher, R.R. (1976) *Implicit Psychology: An Introduction to Social Cognition*, Oxford: Oxford University Press. *Although a little dated, this book provides a thorough introduction to the field of cognitive social psychology.*

8

HOW BRITAIN LOST ITS CONSCIENCE

How Britain lost its conscience

Richard Lynn
© *The Daily Mail*
22/2/93

Something has gone dreadfully wrong with Britain. We have become a helpless society, helpless to confront the crime which makes life a misery in so many parts of our country, helpless to maintain standards of decency, helpless to reverse the trend.

As a modern Professor of Psychology it is not very fashionable to raise the possibility that one of our troubles is a simple lack of conscience. Conscience is one of those words that are taboo in modern psychology because it is not easy to define.

But most people know what it means and I believe that most people would agree lack of conscience is the besetting evil of modern life. (Think of James Bulger; think of the ram-raiders of Sunderland; think of Yasmin Gibson who left her daughter to go on holiday in Spain.)

Ever since 1835, when a Bristol physician identified a condition he termed 'moral imbecility', psychiatrists and psychologists have analysed the processes through which conscience is developed in the human mind.

Conscience is the moral sense. It tells you when you are damaging the people and the world around you. In a more sophisticated way it tells you when you are damaging yourself.

The mark of a person with conscience is self-control. All the latest research shows that the rudiments of self-control are not innate. They are absorbed by children by example and by learning.

Broadly, there are three stages to the learning process. In the first, which lasts until the age of five or six, a child evaluates the morality of behaviour in terms of whether or not he is likely to incur punishment.

Later he realises that society has laws and moral codes to ensure equitable and harmonious behaviour. Then there's a third stage in which moral principles evolve around central beliefs – the equality of human rights, for example, and respect for the dignity of human beings. This is a more flexible morality. There's an understanding by this time that the letter of the law may sometimes be broken in the interests of higher principles.

There is a famous illustration about a man whose wife is dying of cancer, but who might be cured by an expensive drug. The man cannot afford to buy it, so steals a supply. A young child will say that is wrong because people who steal are punished. When he's a little older that same child will say it is wrong because it breaks the law. But the adult believes the theft may be justified because there are exceptional circumstances.

There is evidence to show that children develop a system of morality based on disapproval and punishment and then mature to a more complex morality based on principles of social well-being.

It is widely accepted that children are not born naturally good, as romantic philosophers like Jean-Jacques Rousseau once believed. Children learn their pattern of behaviour from others. The old-fashioned wisdom about the importance of a stable, loving and disciplined home background turns out to have a sound scientific basis.

Postwar psychiatry suggests that there are two major factors which determine whether a child will grow up as a law-abiding member of society or as someone with criminal tendencies – punishment and example.

Punishment is an unpleasant experience which a child's mind will link with wrongdoing. If that child discovers that stealing, swearing or whatever are likely to bring retribution, the chances are that he will avoid such things.

The second factor involves psychological modelling. Children tend to be guided by the behaviour of adults in their family, especially adults of the same sex. Studies by the psychologist Albert Bandura suggest that children are heavily influenced by what they see adults doing. A parent who exhibits an understanding of what is right and what is wrong is likely to bring up a child who has a conscience.

These psychological studies underpin what most responsible parents know instinctively: that it is in the child's own interests and in the interests of his family, to bring him up properly. Unfortunately there may be many families, particularly in the so-called 'underclass', where there is no such awareness.

One explanation for why this underclass is relatively ineffective in bringing up children is that its members have little to lose in terms of social standing or respect if they produce poorly socialised children.

So high levels of crime, drugs, promiscuity and chronic unemployment have become characteristic of inner-city communities. These characteristics are passed from one generation to another by parents.

This may explain the decline in moral values in so many parts of

Europe and America. Parents suffer little or no social disgrace if their children turn out badly.

What can we do about it?

Though there is a good deal of evidence that genetic factors affect people's ability to control their impulses, there is also evidence that young people can be 'conditioned' into good social behaviour.

My view is that the growth of crime in this country is because the concept of punishment has been all but abol- ished. It's unfashionable. It raises lib- eral hackles.

And yet there are scientific reasons to believe that discipline and punish- ment can modify behaviour. Spare the rod and spoil the child may sound des- perately old fashioned, but researchers like John Watson in the early part of this century found that it may be part of the answer. His experimental work with a baby boy called Albert went a long way towards proving that fear does act as a powerful deterrent.

What we need if we are to reverse the present trend is the restoration of stable family life. But that may be a pipedream for the foreseeable future.

In the shorter term, politicians, cler- gymen, the opinion-formers, could do worse than study the conclusions of social science. It might occur to them then that the demand for fair punish- ment is not the reactionary impulse of Colonel Blimp but a response to meticulous research into the make-up of the human mind.

Background

The issue of morality is an important one in psychology since a knowl- edge of its development should provide us with practical ideas about dealing with those moral problems that arise as the result of individual actions. Morality is also a fascinating area since it involves a knowledge of philosophy (to understand the basic concepts involved) and sociol- ogy (to understand individual actions within a social context).

Loosely defined, morality is knowing right from wrong and acting upon this knowledge. This, however, rather begs the question of what is meant by 'right' and 'wrong'. One philosophical approach is to see morals as utilitarian, that is, as social rules and regulations which maintain an effective and well-ordered society. An alternative, so- called deontological, philosophical approach sees morals simply as our duty, laid down by a doctrine or set of principles for action, which can be termed an absolute moral code (Frankena, 1973).

Sociologists take a somewhat different view. Some theorists argue that all moral codes have a functional value in that they serve to main- tain a given society (by, for example, controlling crime) or a social order (by, for example, deference to one's 'betters'). Whatever perspec- tive one adopts, it is unlikely that a universal code of morality either exists or can be established. Since morals certainly vary between differ- ent cultures, their relative nature must always be borne in mind.

Various measures of deviance (violence, theft, and so on) have all shown major and progressive increases over the past 20 years or so (*Social Trends*, 1993). Such an apparent decline in standards has led a number of researchers to investigate its causes, in terms of individual responsibility or general social problems (e.g. Dallos & McLaughlin, 1993). There is evidence which suggests that certain types of problem behaviours can be inherited to some extent (e.g. Thomas & Chess, 1986). However, most research and theories see the development of personal morality as a form of basic socialisation generated from our early environment and learning experiences.

The psychodynamic or Freudian perspective sees morality as the result of a child's identification with its parents, internalising their con- trol as a punitive conscience or as a rewarding ego-ideal. This is sup- posed to happen in order to resolve a psychosexual complex (the

Oedipus complex in boys and the Electra complex in girls) at around five to six years of age. However, whilst a parent's attitudes and beliefs may be very important for a child, there is evidence which indicates that early concepts of right and wrong develop well before the psychodynamic perspective proposes. The complexes themselves are supposed to involve strong (but unconscious) sexual attraction towards the opposite sex parent, although there appears to be little evidence to support this claim (e.g. Hoffman, 1970).

Learning theories also view morality as being a result of past experiences, but suggest that development occurs as a function of the history of the outcomes of our behaviours. Positive outcomes would act as reinforcers for the development of behaviour. For example, a young child given a sweet for helping its mother should be more likely to help (that is, behave pro-socially) in the future. Negative outcomes would act as punishers for our behaviour. A child smacked for bullying a younger sibling should be less likely to engage in this behaviour in the future (but see below for a discussion of the effectiveness of punishment).

The learning theory perspective thus sees morality as simply the result of previous contingencies of reinforcers and punishments. This view, however, lacks the belief that most people seem to have, that morality involves a form of awareness and conscious choice. Eysenck (1970) has attempted to expand the learning theory perspective somewhat to consider the anxiety that is produced by punishment. Eysenck proposes that with repeated learning that involves punishment, a child can become classically conditioned to associate anxiety with the wrongdoing. Eventually, this may even extend to thinking about the activity; the child might then be said to have internalised a sense of what is right (anxiety is not elicited) and what is wrong (anxiety is inhibited).

For some psychologists these approaches are overly mechanistic. Bandura (1973), for example, suggests that much of what we learn as right or wrong is the internalisation of what we observe as appropriate from other people's actions. In one of a series of famous experiments, Bandura and his colleagues demonstrated that when children are shown 'naughty' behaviour being praised, they are more likely to imitate it than if it is punished (Bandura, Ross & Ross, 1963).

Cognitive developmental approaches have also been developed to account for age-related limits to moral reasoning. Piaget (1932) sees mental abilities as becoming progressively more complex in discrete stages. At around five to eight years of age, thought is very self-centred and morality is seen in terms of rules which are fixed and imposed 'from the outside'. At age 10 and beyond, thought incorporates other people and the intentions that underly an action. Moral values are also seen as guidelines to ensure a reasonable social environment. At this stage children are therefore more likely to follow rules by choice.

Kohlberg (1969) has developed these ideas further, and has identified three 'levels' of moral thought. At the 'pre-conventional' level people recognise labels of 'good' and 'bad' and 'right' and 'wrong'. However, these labels are not interpreted in terms of social standards.

Thus, in response to the question, 'Why shouldn't you steal from a store?' a pre-conventional response would be:

'It's not good to steal from the store. It's against the law. Someone could see you and call the police' (Kohlberg, 1976).

At the pre-conventional level, moral judgements are based on the consequences of behaviour. The individual is motivated by personal concerns, initially to avoid punishment and later to obtain reward.

At Kohlberg's second, 'conventional' level, moral judgements are made on the basis of the expectations of the family, social group, or nation at large. In response to the question about stealing from a store, a conventional response would be:

'It's a matter of law. It's one of our rules that we're trying to help to protect everyone. It's something that's needed in our society. If we didn't have these laws, people would steal, they wouldn't have to work for a living and our whole society would get out of kilter' (Kohlberg, 1976).

At this level maintaining conventional expectations has a moral value in its own right.

At the third, 'post-conventional' level, values and principles guide moral judgements, and these transcend the authority of people or conformity to groups. Although people at this level may accept and understand society's rules and laws, they are viewed in terms of their underlying principles which can override conventional rules. According to Kohlberg, this level is reached by relatively few people (such as Mother Teresa). The question about stealing elicited the following response from a person at the post-conventional level:

'It's violating another person's rights, in this case property. (Whilst the law enters into it) the law in most cases is based on what is morally right so it's not a separate subject, it's a consideration. (Morality means) recognising the rights of other individuals, first to life and then to do as he pleases as long as it doesn't interfere with somebody else's rights' (Kohlberg, 1976).

As a psychologist, Lynn's arguments are therefore based on legitimate research findings and carefully formulated theories. These demonstrate that we learn morality from our early social context linked with progressive cognitive maturity. These findings lead Lynn to the conclusion that present social problems are due to a lack of family morality. He infers from this that we therefore need an eventual restoration of 'stable family life' and (more immediately) a social policy of employing 'fair punishment' as a consequence for wrongdoing.

Talking points

1 In the article, Professor Richard Lynn notes that whilst conscience is 'not easy to define ... most people know what it is'. Lynn goes on to define it himself as a sense of morality which leads to self-control. Whilst there is some appeal to Lynn's common-sense approach, it could be very biased and dependent on our specific (Western) culture. Do you think there is a danger that this prevents Lynn from considering other approaches? Are there also categories of social problems which Lynn might define from a common-sense viewpoint that might not lead to further deviance?

Instead of adopting Lynn's approach, one could perhaps take a utilitarian approach and work from a particular 'absolute', such as concern with physical safety. If this approach is taken, should we then be more concerned with violent crime or with the incidence of (say) problems from alcohol abuse and physical damage from smoking cigarettes (both of which are legal activities)?

2 Lynn argues that, 'the growth of crime (in Britain) is because the concept of punishment has been all but abolished.' Quoting 'researchers like John Watson', Lynn suggests that the study of a baby boy called 'Little Albert' (Watson & Rayner, 1920) indicates that 'fear does act as a powerful deterrent'. Although there is evidence to suggest that punishment can be effective, it needs to be prompt, intensive and highly probable (Bower & Hilgard, 1981). There is a lot of evidence, however, that the use of punishment does not deter crime since it is very uncertain and usually delayed.

With respect to social problems, the evidence suggests that many crimes are not even reported to the police and that the 'clear-up' rate for the most frequent categories of offence (such as theft and robbery) is very low (Holdaway, 1988). In behavioural terms this could be described as a very poor training schedule since there is only a weak association between committing a crime and the likelihood of being punished. The evidence about the effectiveness of prisons, for example, indicates that 60 per cent of offenders are back again within four years (Giddens, 1993). Although Lynn would disagree, it could therefore be argued that sending people to prison is actually no better than doing nothing at all. Do you think prisons should be done away with and, if you do, what alternatives to prison could be used instead?

3 In addition to punishment, Lynn also suggests that 'psychological modelling' can be a powerful factor in determining 'whether a child will grow up as a law abiding member of society or as someone with criminal tendencies.' Lynn argues that children tend to be guided by the behaviour of same-sex adults in the family. Research conducted by Bandura and his associates (e.g. Bandura, Ross & Ross, 1963) does suggest that modelling is a plausible explanation for the transmission of social values. Can you think of a situation in which you picked up such concepts from your parents?

Later research has indicated that observational learning also applies to encouraging positive behaviour as well as punishing negative behaviour. A particularly effective approach involves showing someone who is in a situation where they could behave immorally (by, for example, behaving aggressively or stealing) restraining themselves and eventually benefiting from such self-control (Donnerstein & Donnerstein, 1976). How could parents apply this to encourage moral behaviour in their own children?

4 Although Lynn does not directly advocate physical punishment, he comes very close to doing so when he says that 'spare the rod and spoil the child may sound desperately old fashioned but ... it may be part of the answer.' In the home, it may be possible to ensure that the use of physical punishment is fairly consistent, prompt, and at a level that is sufficiently aversive (see Bower & Hilgard, 1981, above).

However, in view of the importance of observational learning it might be asked just what children will learn from this. Punishment also fails to orient children to more positive behaviour; it teaches them what is wrong but does not teach what is right. One consequence of this is that children will seek to avoid being caught rather than generating new behaviours. The punisher (i.e. the parent) also comes to be seen in a negative emotional light, with the result that the prospects of future positive cooperation are correspondingly reduced. Finally, punishment also produces regression – rather than going forward children will, quite logically, return to previous states or strategies which were effective in the past. These may give rise to even more problems.

In view of the above, do you think parents should ever smack their children? If not, what should they do instead? Surely it is better to administer a brief physical punishment rather than a long-term psychological one, isn't it?

5 Many theorists (including Lynn) talk about a feckless and immoral 'underclass' who 'have little to lose in terms of social standing or respect if they produce poorly socialised children.' Murray (1990) in particular has partly attributed this development to the rise in single-parent families, something which has more than doubled in the UK over the last 20 years. As the vast majority of these single parents are women, the argument is that the firm control and moral values that a father would bring are lacking. Such families are undoubtedly under a wide range of pressures to cope. Do you think it is fair to blame the apparent ills of society upon them? Some American states have gone so far as to refuse welfare assistance for the subsequent children of such women. What do you think the effects of this policy will be on society?

6 A perspective from social psychology proposes that much of our behaviour can be explained as 'self-presentation'. According to Goffman (1969), people form a concept of how they wish others to perceive them (and this is incorporated into the self-concept). They then behave in a way which is consistent with this. Goffman suggests that our ideas of what we wish to present vary according to the situation in which we find ourselves. Thus, a nurse wearing a uniform is much more likely to go to help after an accident than a nurse not in uniform.

Our sense of self-identity can be seen as arising from the groups (or social structures) that we are a part of (Tajfel, 1982). Membership of a gang, for example, has been shown to generate powerful norms or expectancies of behaviour that can lead to deviance (Whyte, 1943). Behaviour which society labels as a 'problem' or 'immoral' can therefore be seen as rational attempts by individuals to define and present their self-concept to other people.

Although writers such as Lynn correlate an increase in immorality (as measured by rising crime statistics) with a lack of family morality (as indicated by the rise in single-parent families), a correlation does not necessarily mean that a change in one of these measures causes a change in the other. In recent years there has been a variety of major changes in both the social climate and statistics such as the level of employment. How might these operate to generate a climate in which deviant behaviour might form and flourish? Why might it be difficult for psychologists like Lynn to acknowledge the importance of such general social factors?

7 In suggesting that 'the rudiments of self-control [and hence morality] . . . are absorbed by children by example and by learning'. Lynn draws on Kohlberg's (1969) research on moral development. Although Kohlberg's research has been influential, it has been criticised on the grounds that it is derived from studies of moral reasoning rather than moral actions. Kohlberg arrived at his theory by giving young boys 'moral dilemmas' (such as that described by Lynn). The judgement of the moral stage people have predominantly achieved is based on their reasoning about what they say they would do. When actual behaviour is studied in different situations, such as the home and school, behaviour seems to be to some extent specific to that particular context (e.g. Hartshorne & May, 1930). In what other ways can Kohlberg's theory be criticised? Do you agree with Kohlberg that moral progress occurs when people are exposed to more advanced moral reasoning applied in the context of problem situations? Would real-life moral decisions be more effective in promoting progress than moral dilemmas?

References and further reading

Those references which are particularly worthy of further reading are indicated thus: *, together with a brief description of their area of concern.

Bandura, A. (1973) *Aggression: A Social Learning Analysis*, New Jersey: Prentice-Hall.

*Bandura, A., Ross, D., & Ross, S.A. (1963) 'Imitation of film-mediated aggressive models', *Journal of Abnormal and Social Psychology*, 66, pp. 3–11. *A classic study showing the power of observational learning.*

Bower, G. & Hilgard, E. (1981) *Theories of Learning*, New Jersey: Prentice-Hall.

*Dallos, R. & McLaughlin, E. (1993) *Social Problems and the Family*, London: Sage Publications. *Chapter 5 gives a good overview of sociological issues in juvenile delinquency.*

Donnerstein, E. & Donnerstein, M. (1976) 'Research in the control of interracial aggression', **in** R. Geen & E. O'Neil (Eds.), *Perspectives on Aggression*, New York: Academic Press.

Eysenck, H.J. (1970) *Crime and Personality*, London: Paladin.

*Frankena, W. (1973) *Ethics*, New Jersey: Prentice-Hall. *Frankena's book provides a useful introduction to the philosophy of morality.*

Giddens, A. (1993) *Sociology*, Cambridge: Polity Press.

Goffman, E. (1969) *The Presentation of Self in Everyday Life*, Harmondsworth: Penguin.

Hartshorne, H. & May, M. (1930) *Studies in the Nature of Character*, New York: Macmillan.

Hoffman, M. (1970 'Conscience, personality and socialisation techniques', *Human Development*, 13, pp. 90–126.

Holdaway, S. (1988) *Crime and Deviance*, London: Macmillan.

*Kohlberg, L. (1969) *Stages in the Development of Moral Thought and Action*, New York: Holt, Reinhart & Winston. *This is Kohlberg's original description of his stage theory of moral development.*

Kohlberg, L. (1976) 'Moral Stages and Moralisation: The Cognitive-Developmental Approach', **in** T. Lickona (Ed.), *Moral Development and Behaviour: Theory, Research and Social Issues*, New York: Holt, Rinehart & Winston.

*Kohlberg, L. (1981) *The Philosophy of Moral Development: Moral Stages and the Idea of Justice*, San Francisco: Harper & Row. *Whilst Kohlberg's (1969) publication describes in detail his early research, this publication provides an excellent overview of the ways in which research in this area has developed.*

Murray, C. (1990) *The Emerging British Underclass*, London: Institute of Economic Affairs.

Piaget, J. (1932) *The Moral Judgement of the Child*, London: Routledge and Kegan Paul.

Social Trends (1993) *Volume 23*, London: H.M.S.O.

Tajfel, H. (1982) *Social Identity and Intergroup Relations*, Cambridge: Cambridge University Press.

Thomas, A. & Chess, S. (1986) 'The New York longitudinal study: From infancy to early adult life', **in** R. Plomin & J. Dunn (Eds.) *The Study of Temperament*, Hillsdale, New Jersey: Earlbaum.

Watson, J.B. & Rayner, R. (1920) 'Conditional emotional reactions', *Journal of Experimental Psychology*, 3, pp. 1–14.

Whyte, W. (1943) *Street Corner Society: The Social Structure of an Italian Slum*, Chicago: The University of Chicago Press.

9

GRIT YOUR TEETH AND ENJOY IT

Grit your teeth and enjoy it

Sharon Kingman
© *The Independent on Sunday*
2/12/90

If you had mentioned the word dentist to Christine Higgs a year ago, she would have 'crawled up the wall'. Now she finds going to the dentist such a pleasant experience that she will miss her regular visits when she finishes her course of treatment.

After 13 years during which she could not bring herself to visit a dentist, she finds her change of attitude – achieved with the help of therapy – hard to believe. Not everybody is so lucky. Studies have shown that one in 10 people do not go to the dentist at all because they are so frightened; one in three of those who do go are so terrified that they are difficult to treat.

Jennifer Pinder, the dentist who eventually treated Christine, points out that there is a whole spectrum of nervousness associated with going to the dentist. Some people feel mildly apprehensive; others may find that just making a phone call to the surgery can bring on a panic attack.

The causes are just as variable: one patient of Jennifer Pinder's had been slapped by her previous dentist and told not to be so stupid. Another man had a fear of injections after having a cholera shot while abroad. The needles used were so old and blunt that it took four attempts to complete the injection. Nervous parents will often transmit their fears to a child.

Christine cannot identify the exact moment her problem began. During the seventies she had dental treatment a couple of times, but only with the help of intravenously administered sedatives. The first injection knocked her out, but she came round during the second. After that she could not even cope with making a dental appointment, and knew that even if someone else made the appointment for her, she would never go.

Last year, the full extent of her phobia came home to her. She heard a dentist's drill while listening to a tape at work. She started hyperventilating and said she could not complete the typing. It took her 24 hours to recover her emotional equilibrium.

After mentioning the problem to her GP she was referred to Dr Stan Lindsay, a clinical psychologist at the Institute of Psychiatry in London, who specialises in people with severe dental phobias. Fear of pain is the most common complaint, says Dr Lindsay, followed by dread of fainting, choking and being trapped. Some people fear injections or, like Christine Higgs, the drill.

At Christine's first appoiintment, Dr Lindsay asked her if she could pick up a syringe, a dental mirror and two probing instruments. One of these was pointed, and she could only hold it at arm's length. Afterwards, she could not stop shaking.

Dr Lindsay says: 'We get them used to the sights, sounds and sensations of dental treatment, by gradually exposing them to the sorts of things that terrify them.' An important part of the therapy is instruction in how to relax.

When Dr Lindsay first played Christine a tape of a dentist's drill she could only bear to hear it for a few seconds before it was turned off and she tried to calm herself down with relaxation exercises. But within a few months, she found she was able to tolerate bursts of 15 minutes or more.

Jennifer Pinder, who collaborates with Dr Lindsay, started to see Christine about halfway through her therapy. The first appointment involved only a chat; the second just an X-ray. Only then did they start to discuss dental treatment.

Christine, who started therapy last December, set herself goals. 'It sounds daft to want to go to the dentist on your birthday, but I had three fillings done that day.' By August, when she had booked a holiday, she had four new crowns on her front teeth.

What advice would she give to someone in a similar situation? 'It took me a good 10 years to admit to the problem. The thing is that you've got to want to get help.'

Dr Lindsay points out that the treatment Christine Higgs had is available on the NHS, although clinical psychologists are scarce and there is often a waiting list. He suggests initially contacting the local community health council.

People with less severe dental phobia may ring the dental helpline run by the British Dental Health Foundation. Ian Robertson, who runs the service, has had about 5 000 calls since it began four years ago.

About half were from people who are frightened of going to the dentist. Some have rung in tears; others have resorted to pulling out their own teeth with pliers.

'It helps people to understand that they are not the only ones, and that there are ways of overcoming their fears', Mr Robertson says. Fear of dentists has nothing to do with weakness of character: Mr Robertson says he has come across dental phobics in senior positions in business, the police force and the fire service, some of them with awards for bravery. Often, he says, the problem can be solved by finding a sympathetic dentist.

John Tiernan, also of the British Dental Health Foundation, urges people to be consumerist. 'Phone the practice first and tell them you are nervous. If you get the "don't be silly" attitude at the end of the phone, then try somewhere else'.

'If you just say, "Do you deal with nervous patients?" most practices would say "yes". But if you say, "I can't walk past your practice without feeling ill, can you help me?" you are more likely to find out the true response of the practice.'

John Tiernan uses hypnosis to help anxious patients – he describes it as a kind of controlled daydreaming – and frequently manages to begin treatment, with the patient's approval, on the first visit. People with very deep-rooted fear may take longer to relax.

For them, the best strategy may be to book for a consultation and not for treatment, John Tiernan says. He also advises people to seek treatment before they are in pain. If a tooth has been aching for several days, good pain relief can be difficult.

One of the dentist's most important roles is to enable the patient to feel in control. Jennifer Pinder says 'We tell them, "If you feel any discomfort, raise your right hand and we will stop immediately." That control makes them feel less helpless. But as a dentist, you have to keep your word and stop and find out what the problem is.'

Background

In a study carried out 22 years after the introduction of the National Health Service (NHS), Gray, Todd, Slack and Bulman (1970) reported that 45 per cent of adults aged 16 or more were endentulous, that is, had none of their natural teeth. Although 45 per cent of Gray and his colleagues' sample had lost their teeth prior to the introduction of the NHS, under half of a sub-sample aged 16 to 34 who had received NHS treatment for most of their lives admitted to attending check-ups regularly.

More surprisingly, a further 41.3 per cent confessed to the researchers that they only visited the dentist when they had trouble with their teeth or when the pain had become so great that it could not be tolerated any further. Given the fact that under the NHS conservative dentistry was available to all, and numerous advertising campaigns stressed the point that regular check-ups were essential to the maintenance of good oral hygiene, the findings reported by Gray and his colleagues were treated with incredulity.

In a very early investigation of dental attenders, Friedson and Feldman (1958) examined the reasons why a substantial proportion of the general public do not attend the dentist's on a regular, or even irregular, basis. The findings showed that some people attributed their non-attendance to 'laziness' or 'having no need to go'. However, the findings also showed that a significant number of people of all ages and all social classes attributed their non-attendance to a fear of dentists and dentistry in general and certain aspects of dental treatment in particular.

Since the publication of Friedson and Feldman's research, a number of other studies have been conducted. In one, Curson and Caplans (1970) reported that at least 38 per cent of the patients who were attending the emergency clinic in an inner London hospital were too afraid to visit a dentist except in an emergency. More recent research (e.g. Todd & Walker, 1980; Green & Green, 1985) has reported similar findings, and it has been estimated that 'between a quarter and a third of adults experience high levels of fear during routine dental treatment' (Lindsay & Jackson, 1993). Specific dental procedures which have been shown to elicit particularly high levels of fear are anaesthesia, injections and the sight, sound and feel of the high speed dentist's drill (Kleinknecht, Klepac & Alexander, 1973). In one study (Ship & White, 1968) it was demonstrated that operative procedures produced greater biochemical changes indicative of stress than prophylaxis, oral examination or X-ray.

Todd and Walker's (1980) national survey of dental health in England and Wales painted as bleak a picture as the findings reported by Gray, et al. (1970). They found that 59 per cent of adults with some teeth were found on examination to have some active decay, and that dental health was significantly poorer in patients who sought treatment only when in pain compared with those who regularly visited the dentist.

Perhaps ironically, given what has just been said above, one of the reasons why some people appear to be frightened of visiting the dentist's is the expectation of pain. In an attempt to investigate the contribution of the expectation of pain to fear of dentistry, Wardle (1982) interviewed two groups of patients who were about to undergo some form of dental treatment. Both regular and irregular attenders were interviewed. Wardle's first group of interviewees were patients waiting for X-rays to be developed prior to undergoing a variety of procedures. The second group were attending the dentist's specifically to receive one or more fillings preceded by an injection.

Both groups were asked to provide reasons for their dental anxiety and to rate a list of dental procedures for **a)** their perceived 'fearfulness' and **b)** their perceived 'painfulness'. Those patients awaiting fillings were additionally requested to rate the anxiety and pain they expected to experience in the treatment they were about to undergo. As with other studies, Wardle's results showed that fear of pain was the major source of dental anxiety. The data also revealed that there were high correlations of ratings of pain and anxiety for most dental procedures, with those perceived as being more painful eliciting more anxiety. Wardle's third major finding was that those who considered themselves 'fearless' expected to experience less pain than those who considered themselves 'fearful'. On the basis of these results, Wardle concluded that the expectation of pain makes a significant contribution to dental anxiety.

The question that arises as a result of these findings is why the dentally fearful person expects to experience pain. Melamed (1979) argues that anxiety aroused by dentistry is different from other clinical anxieties because its characteristics are rational, that is, there actually is the possibility of experiencing discomfort at the dentist's. It has been shown that the most common cause identified for the onset of dental fear is traumatic experience during dental treatment with, in one study (Moore, Brodsgard & Birn, 1991), 86 per cent of dentally fearful patients falling into this category.

In an early major study of fear of the dentist's, Lautch (1971) reported that in a group of patients who were extremely anxious about attending the dentist's, every one reported having had at least one traumatic experience when they had visited the dentist's during childhood. On the basis of this, Lautch offered a straightforward simultaneous classical conditioning explanation for the occurrence of dental anxiety.

According to this, pain acts as an unconditional stimulus which reflexively produces an unconditional response of fear. The simultaneous sound of the drill, (the conditional stimulus) accompanying painful contact of the drill with a tooth, produces an association between the presence of the drill (its sight, sound and feel) and the expectation of a painful experience, with the result that fear (the conditional response) is elicited. Support for this account can be adduced from research reported by Woolgrave, Atkins and Cumberbatch (1980), who showed that patients asked to explain their fear of the dentist's did so in terms of the anticipatory fear of being subjected to a painful experience.

Until recently, the potential application of psychological knowledge and research to dentistry has been largely ignored. For example, the Nuffield Report on Dental Education (Thomas, 1980) suggested that applied psychology had no place on the dental curriculum. As a result, people who were particularly frightened of the dentist's had typically to seek the help of a dentist who they had heard was particularly tolerant and helpful and/or would provide general anaesthesia for dental surgery.

In 1990, however, the General Dental Council formally recognised the contribution which the behavioural sciences can make to the practice of dentistry in general and the investigation and treatment of dental fear in particular (Lindsay & Jackson, 1993). As Lindsay and Woolgrave (1982) have observed, 'with a measure of enterprise, clinical psychology can contribute significantly to the management of fear and pain in dentistry.'

Talking points

1 As noted in the **Background**, a large percentage of adults in Great Britain fear dental treatment. This phenomenon has also been observed in other countries. For example, a study undertaken in the Netherlands by Schurrs, Duivenvoorden, Van Velze and Verhage (1981) indicated that 36 per cent of a large and representative sample 'dreaded' visits to the dentist. Many studies use questionnaires or interviews as their method of data collection. Why might such methods give an inaccurate description of the intensity of fear reported by people? Perhaps a more accurate assessment of fear of dentistry could be obtained using behavioural measures. What aspects of Christine Higgs' behaviour described in the article could be used to support the view that her intensity of fear is such that the term 'dental phobic' is not inappropriate?

2 One behavioural measure that can be used to assess fear is the extent to which it leads a person to avoid visiting the dentist's. Christine Higgs, for example, 'could not even cope with making a dental appointment, and knew that even if someone else made the appointment for her, she would never go.' However, data exist which suggests that those who are the most fearful of dental procedures (without actually being phobic) are also amongst the most likely to attend a dentist's regularly (Liddell & May, 1984). As Liddell and May have remarked, fear of dentistry does not always act as a strong deterrent in every case

in which it occurs. Why do you think the most fearful would also be among the most likely regular attenders? What cautions should be exercised when the measure of attendance at the dentist's is used as an index of fear?

3 According to Lautch's straightforward simultaneous classical conditioning explanation for fear of dentistry, those who could be considered 'phobic' would be expected to have had one or more frightening dental experiences in the past. Such experiences could include sudden and unpredictable pain from the failure of local or general anaesthesia (as described in the article) and procedures such as the 'hand over the mouth exercise' (Weinstein & Domoto, 1992). What support does the article provide for a classical conditioning account of fear of dentistry?

Although some evidence can be used to support an account of dental fear based on classical conditioning, there is evidence against this approach to the understanding of dental fear. For example, in at least one study (Liddell & May, 1984) both regular and irregular dental attenders had experienced painful episodes in the past. What other evidence would argue against a classical conditioning explanation?

4 Even if there was a very strong link between the experience of fear and the previous experience of pain in identical circumstances, such an observation would only be correlational and not causal. What other factors might contribute to fear of dentistry? Can you design a study to assess the alleged causal link between fear and the previous experience of pain? Would you anticipate any ethical questions arising if such a study was designed and planned to be carried out?

5 Dr Lindsay's treatment of Christine Higgs appears to have been so successful that 'now she finds going to the dentist's such a pleasant experience ... she will miss her regular visits when she finishes the course of treatment.' Although there may be some debate over the role of classical conditioning in the development of fear of dentistry, it is clear from the article that Dr Lindsay is using some sort of therapeutic approach based on conditioning principles. Which major type of behaviour therapy is Lindsay's technique closest to, and on what conditioning principle does it appear to be based? Could any other behavioural therapies be used to treat those people afraid of the dentist's? Would the application of these give rise to any ethical issues? What other psychological techniques could be used to treat those fearful of dentistry?

6 In adults, fear of dentistry is typically characterised by a high degree of apprehensiveness and the avoidance of dental appointments. In children, fear is expressed more in terms of behaviour in the dentist's chair. Thus, pushing away the dentist and closing the mouth at an inappropriate time (such as when an injection is about to be given) are both characteristic of fear (Lindsay, Roberts & Gibson, 1978). Shoben & Borland (1954) have suggested that the attitudes and experiences of a person's family in relation to dentistry are the most important in determining a child's reaction to attending the dental surgery.

Although a re-analysis of Shoben and Borland's data (Forgione &

Clark, 1974) has indicated that they overestimated the importance of family attitudes and experiences, the family (especially, it would seem, the mother of the child: Gershen, 1976) undoubtedly plays some sort of a role. Does the article lend any credence to this view, and what sorts of processes may lead to a child developing a fear of the dentist? How could a dentist reduce a child's fear?

7 The article suggests that 'one of the most important roles (of the dentist) is to enable the patient to feel in control.' One way of achieving this is through the use of what are called 'stop signals'. As the article indicates: 'We tell (patients), "if you feel any discomfort, raise your right hand and we will stop immediately". That control makes them feel less helpless.'

Similar strategies are used in other settings where patients are receiving physical treatment. The strategies have the effect of minimising the mismatch between expectations and experiences, and encourage cognitive activity of a 'coping' rather than 'catastrophising' kind (Chaves & Brown, 1978). What other strategies could dentists use to provide patients with more control over the situation? Aside from pain-free dentistry (which is impossible to achieve), what other strategies could be used to minimise the experience of anxiety about the receipt of dental treatment?

8 Some studies have revealed a variety of demographic differences between dental attenders and non-attenders. In one of these (Biro & Hewson, 1976), women and younger children were found to attend more regularly than men and older people, whilst higher income, education and social position were also shown to be positively related to the seeking of regular dental care. In Gray et al.'s (1970) study, adults living in London and the South-East were more likely to visit their dentist on a regular basis than adults in the North of the country. How would you explain the apparent geographical differences? (Your answer to this may be affected by whether you come from the North or South-East of the country!)

9 The article uses the term 'dental phobic' to describe people like Christine Higgs. A phobic disorder is one in which a person has an excessive, irrational, fear of objects, situations or activities which cause significant distress and which may be so great that the person goes to great lengths to avoid the phobic object, situation or activity, and this interferes with normal everyday functioning. Although there may be some disagreement as to whether fear of the dentist's can properly be described as a phobia (e.g. Melamed, 1979), assume that it is. If claustrophobia is fear of enclosed spaces and astrophobia fear of thunder and lightning, what is 'dental phobia'?

References and further reading

Those references which are particularly worthy of further attention are indicated thus: *, together with a brief description of their area of concern.

Biro, P.A. & Hewson, N.D. (1976) 'A survey of patients' attitudes towards their dentist', *Australian Dental Journal*, 21, pp. 388–94.

Chaves, J.F. & Brown, J.M. (1978) 'Self-generated strategies for the control of pain and stress', paper presented to the APA, Toronto, Canada.

Curson, I. & Caplans, M.P. (1970) 'The need for sedation in conservative dentistry', *British Dental Journal*, 128, pp. 19–32.

Forgione, A.G. & Clark, R.E. (1974) 'Comments on the empirical study of the causes of dental fear', *Journal of Dental Research*, 53, p. 496.

Friedson, E. & Feldman, J.J. (1958) 'The public looks at dental care', *Journal of the American Dental Association*, 67, pp. 90–8.

Gershen, J.A. (1976) 'Maternal influence on the behaviour patterns of children in dental situations', *Journal of Dentistry for Children*, 43, pp. 28–32.

Gray, P.G., Todd, J.E., Slack, G.L. & Bulman, J.S. (1970) *Adult Dental Health in England and Wales in 1968*, London: H.M.S.O.

Green, R.M. & Green, A. (1985) 'Adult attitudes to dentistry among dental attenders in South Wales', *British Dental Journal*, 158, pp. 157–60.

Kleinknecht, R.A., Klepac, R.K. & Alexander, L.D. (1973) 'Origins and characteristics of fear of dentistry', *Journal of the American Dental Association*, 86, pp. 842–8.

*Lautch, H. (1971) 'Dental phobia', *British Journal of Psychiatry*, 119, pp. 151–8. *An excellent review of early research in the area, together with a full account of Lautch's attempt to account for dental phobia in classical conditioning terms.*

Liddell, A. & May, B. (1984) 'Some characteristics of regular and irregular attenders for dental check-ups', *British Journal of Clinical Psychology*, 23, pp. 19–26.

*Lindsay, S.J.E. & Woolgrave, J.C. (1982) 'Fear and pain in dentistry', *Bulletin of the British Psychological Society*, 35, pp. 225–8. *This article includes a review of some of the issues that have attracted the attention of those psychologists interested in this area.*

*Lindsay, S.J.E. & Jackson, C.P. (1993) 'Fear of routine dental treatment in adults: Its nature and management', *Psychology and Health*, 8, pp. 135–53. *An up-to-date review article summarising most of the available evidence on fear of dentistry.*

Lindsay, S.J.E., Roberts, G.J. & Gibson, A. (1978) 'The techniques of O-NO sedation', *Proceedings of the British Paedodontic Society*, 8, pp. 13–15.

*Melamed, B.G. (1979) 'Behavioural approaches to fear in dental settings', *Progress in Behaviour Modification*, 7, pp. 171–203. *A review* *of some of the ways in which psychological treatment methods can be applied to fear of dentistry.*

Moore, R., Brodsgard, I. & Birn, H. (1991) 'Manifestations, acquisition and diagnostic categories of dental fear in a self-referred population', *Behaviour Research and Therapy*, 29, pp. 51–60.

Ship, I.I. & White, C.L. (1968) 'Physiologic response to dental stress', *Oral Surgery, Oral Medicine and Oral Pathology*, 13, pp. 368–75.

Shoben, E.J. & Borland, L. (1954) 'An empirical study of the aetiology of dental fears', *Journal of Clinical Psychology*, 10, pp. 171–4.

Schurrs, A.H.B., Duivenvoorden, H., Van Velzen, S. & Verhage, F. (1981) *Factors Associated with Regularity of Dental Attendance: An Empirical-Psychological Investigation*, Brussels: Stafleu & Tholen.

Thomas, T.C. (1980) *Dental Education: The Report of a Committee of Inquiry*, London: Nuffield Foundation.

Todd, J.E. & Walker, J. (1980) *Adult Dental Health in England and Wales*, London, HMSO.

*Wardle, J. (1982) 'Fear of dentistry', *British Journal of Medical Psychology*, 55, pp. 119–26. *Wardle's study is an excellent example of empirical research using the interview method.*

Weinstein, P. & Domoto, P. (1992) 'Positive and aversive management procedures and their impact: Lessons from research and a dental fear clinic at the University of Washington', *International Journal of Paediatric Dentistry*, 2, p. 58.

Woolgrave, J.C., Atkins, J. & Cumberbatch, N.G. (1980) 'Will it hurt? Pain and fear in the dentist's chair', paper presented at the British Association for the Advancement of Science, Salford.

10

THE MAN WHO HAS MEMORISED THE PHONE BOOK AND OTHER STORIES

The man who has memorised the phone book, and other stories

Ben Macintyre
© *The Observer*

A small but notable hiccup interrupted the first world memory championship (or Memoriad) yesterday when the host, Barry Buzan, forgot he was wearing a microphone and walked in front of a loudspeaker, thus partially deafening half the audience with feedback. It was practically the only thing forgotten by anyone during the entire event.

The championship, in which contestants proved their ability to absorb a breathtaking quantity of more or less useless information, was held at the Athenaeum Club, in Pall Mall – not a place immediately associated with great feats of memory. The doorman couldn't remember what time the event started, or what it was about.

Mr Buzan, according to his assistant, is a genius, a visionary, the most creative man on earth, and author of 11 books (with 29 more pending) on how to improve your memory.

A dapper man, who looks like Johnny Carson and sounds like Alistair Cooke, he began the proceedings with a test: the audience was asked to list the first eight planets in orbit around the sun, in their correct order, no conferring. When some people failed to score anything at all, Mr Buzan was triumphant. 'It's socially painful, personally embarrassing, isn't it?'

It is, of course, nothing of the sort, but Mr Buzan has an interest in promoting the idea that people who can't remember things they could quite easily look up are inferior, since he runs several centres in Britain and America that aim to 'increase the hidden potential of the human brain'. His video on the subject sells for £299, plus VAT. The rich and powerful care about memory, he insists, but nobody reminded him of Ronald...erm... Reagan.

Comparing the Memoriad with the Olympics, Mr Buzan announced that yesterday's event, 'a moment in history, the first time in the world that people have gathered together to look at memory', would set benchmarks for the future.

We sat breathless and cowed while he revealed the mind-numbing fact that Hideaki Tomoyori of Japan had succeeded in memorising pi to 40 000 decimal places. The national champion of pi memorisation, Mr Creighton Carvello was then introduced; he had managed to recite 20 013 digits over a period of nine hours and 10 minutes.

Mr Carvello, a psychiatric nurse, is currently learning by heart the entire Cleveland area telephone directory. He claims he has mastered 24 000 numbers so far, including all the Smiths. It took him just four seconds to come up with the correct number for one A.D. Smith of Middlesborough.

Leaving aside the question of whether it is sensible to employ someone as a psychiatric nurse who may, at any moment, tell you the telephone number of someone you don't know, Mr Carvello is a dedicated man, spending three or four hours a day curled up with the directory.

'Whatever the champions can do, basically anyone can do', said Mr Buzan, which still left open the burning question of why anyone should want to.

Whatever their motivation, the memory giants at the Athenaeum have chalked up some remarkable feats: Dominic O'Brien holds the record for recalling the correct order of several packs of shuffled cards. In 1990 he corectly remembered the exact sequence of 25 packs, a record he hopes to break this year.

David Norwood gave a demonstration of blindfold chess. Dr Elizabeth Valentine, a lecturer at the University of London, read a short address entitled 'Tom Morton: a living telephone directory'.

Tom Morton's technique involves associating pairs of numbers with visual images: 57 with a bottle of Heinz tomato ketchup, 49 wth his mother (her age when he started the technique) and bicycle with 00. Thus when he thinks of the number 574900, he imagines his mother riding on a bicycle with a bottle of tomato sauce. This left some members of the audience baffled and depressed. They cheered up, however, when informed that minutes after being read a story about Africa, Tom Morton could barely remember any of it.

Background

Techniques for aiding recall from memory, which most people consider to be unusual and artificial, are termed mnemonics (the word mnemonic derives from Mnemosyne, the Greek goddess of memory). Mnemonic devices have two fundamental characteristics according to Belezza (1981). First, they are not inherently connected to the material that has to be learned. Instead, they impose meaning and structure on material that is otherwise not very meaningful or structured. Second, they typically involve adding something to the material to create meaningful associations between what is to be learned and what is already stored in long-term memory.

Mnemonic devices do not therefore simplify information, but make it more elaborate with the result that more, rather than less, information is stored in memory. However, the additional information makes the material easier to recall and the mnemonic device organises new information into a cohesive whole so that the retrieval of part of the information ensures the retrieval of the rest of it (Carlson, 1988).

Although commercial packages promising memory improvement may be a relatively recent phenomenon, the use of mnemonic devices is not. Writing in the first century BC, Cicero tells the story of the Greek poet Simonides who lived around 500 BC. Evidently Simonides was invited to attend a banquet and give a recitation in honour of the victor of an Olympian wrestling match. Shortly after his speech, Simonides left the banqueting hall just moments before the walls, floor and ceiling collapsed, killing many of the guests. Such was the destruction that most of the guests were unrecognisable. Simonides, however,was able to identify the victims by imagining himself back in the banqueting hall and remembering that one person was sitting by a certain doorway, another by a particular column, and so on.

Simonides later applied this system to remembering other things. Whenever he wanted to remember a list of items he would visualise a building and then imagine the items in various locations, usually starting with the door of the building. When Simonides needed to recall the items he would imagine each of the locations in sequence, 'picture' the item stored in a location, and then say it. In order to store a speech, Simonides could group the words into concepts and leave a 'note' for each concept at a particular location in the sequence (Yates, 1966).

Simonides' 'method of loci' (loci is Greek for 'places') became popular with classical orators and is still used by people today in various forms. A variation of this mnemonic device is called the 'narrative story' method. Its effectiveness as a mnemonic device has been demonstrated experimentally by Bower and Clark (1969). In their study, one group of participants were simply instructed to try to learn 12 lists of 10 concrete nouns. Participants in the other group were advised to:

> Make up a story relating the items to one another. Start with the first item and put it in a setting which will allow other items to be added to it. Then, add the other items to the story in the same order as they appear in the list. Make each story meaningful to yourself. When you are asked to recall the items, you can simply go through your story and pull out the items in their correct order.

Although both groups of participants could remember a given list equally well immediately after its presentation, the performance of the group that constructed narrative stories was overwhelmingly superior when recall of all 120 words was tested.

Mnemonic devices are not simply limited to the learning of lists of words. For example, Snowman, Krebs and Lockhart (1980) taught college students on a 'study skills' course to use the loci method to remember the central concepts from a 2 200 word passage of prose. As compared with students taught more traditional study skills, the group that used the loci method recalled significantly more ideas from the passage. The loci method has also been used successfully by special populations such as the blind, brain damaged and elderly (e.g. Yesavage & Rose, 1984).

In addition to Simonides' method and the variations on it, there are many other mnemonic devices that can be used as aids to recall. One of these, which also uses imagery, is called the 'key' or 'peg' word system and was introduced to England in the late nineteenth century by John Sambrook (Paivio, 1979). A rhyme such as 'one is a bun, two is a shoe, three is a tree' and so on, is used to associate an object (the key or peg word) with each number in the rhyme. The items to be remembered are then individually paired with a key word by means of a mental image. For example, if the first word to be remembered is 'clock', an image of a bun with a clock face might be formed. For each of the items the rhyme is recited and the mental image previously formed is 'triggered' with the result that the item is recalled.

A mnemonic device similar to the key word method was devised by Henry Herdson in the seventeenth century (Hunter, 1957). Herdson's method involved imagining numbers as objects. Thus, 1 might be imagined as a pencil, 2 as a swan, and so on. The items to be remembered are then imagined interacting with their relevant number. For example, if the item to be remembered was 'clock', an image of a clock with a pencil for the minute hand might be formed.

Yet another method using imagery has been devised by Laird Cermak (1978) and is called 'mediation'. In this method, two items are linked with a third that ties them together. For example, suppose that the two items to be remembered are the names Bill and Peter. Cermak suggests that it would be possible to mediate between the two by linking Bill with electricity (as in electricity bill) and Peter with the rhyming word meter. The mediation would be 'Bill-electricity-meter-Peter'.

Perhaps the most famous mnemonist of all who relied on imagery was a Russian newspaper reporter called Shereshevskii (or 'S') studied by Alexander Luria (1968). S's memory appeared to have no limits and included the ability to recall lists of more than a hundred digits and elaborate scientific formulae, even though he was not a scientist. One of the strategies used by S was the 'narrative story' method outlined earlier:

When S read through a long series of words, each word would elicit a graphic image, and since the series was fairly long, he had to find some way of distributing these images in a mental row or sequence. Most often (and this habit persisted throughout his life) he would 'distribute' them along some roadway or street he visualised in his mind ... Frequently he would take a mental walk along that street ... and slowly make his way down, 'distributing' his images at houses, gates, and in store windows ... This technique of converting a series of words into a series of graphic images explains why S could so readily reproduce a series from start to finish or in reverse order; how he could rapidly name the word that preceded or followed one I'd selected from the series. To do this he would simply begin his walk, either from the beginning or end of the street, find the image of the object I had named and 'take a look at' whatever happened to be situated on either side of it. (Luria, 1968)

Apparently, S was capable of recalling things he had been asked to remember when he was retested 15 years later!

Talking points

1 Although the role of imagery in improving memory has a long history, Allan Paivio (1971) was the psychologist primarily responsible for regenerating experimental interest in it. Try the following demonstration of visual imagery. Without thinking, estimate the number of windows you have in your house. Now form a mental image of your house. Starting at the front door, walk through the house in a systematic manner, counting the windows as your enter various rooms. How close was your initial estimate to your imagined estimate, and which is closest to the actual number of windows?

The number of windows in a house is not likely to be 'routinely available' since most of us do not commit such trivial facts to memory, so you should have found that the imagined estimate was closest. Why do you think visual imagery can improve memory for verbal material? Why do you think imagery is best suited for representing 'concrete' rather than abstract events, objects and words? What would you do if you wanted to store abstract verbal material in imaginal form?

2 Tom Morton ('the living telephone directory' according to the article) uses what seems to be a mixture of the visual imagery mnemonics described in the **Background**. According to Lorayne and Lucas (1974), 'in order to remember any new piece of information it must be remembered with something you already know or remember, in some ridiculous way'. The implication is that 'bizarreness' is one of the factors that makes visual imagery effective. Why should an image's bizarreness make it more effective? What other factors do you think can help to make visual association effective? Can you design a study to test the hypothesis that visual imagery is effective as a mnemonic device? What sorts of confounding errors might occur in your study and are there any individual differences you would need to control for?

3 The method of loci requires the learner to memorise mental images of familiar locations in some natural or logical order. The locations become what Higbee (1989) has termed 'the mental filing system' which can be used repeatedly for different lists of items that need to be committed to memory. Psychologists still cannot explain satisfactorily why the ancient Greek orators did not confuse sequences from different speeches. How do you think interference effects were avoided?

Suppose a person used his or her six-roomed house as the loci, but needed to remember a list containing 36 items. How could that person adapt the loci system to enable this task to be achieved? One disadvantage of the method of loci would seem to be that a person cannot directly retrieve, say, the eleventh item on a list since the preceding 10 loci must be counted before the eleventh can be identified. Can you think of a tactic a mnemonist could use to greatly reduce the 'search time' necessary to identify a particular item?

4 Higbee (1989) distinguishes between visual mnemonic systems (using visual imagery and as described in the **Background**) and verbal mnemonic techniques, which make associations with words. Verbal mnemonics include rhyming ('In fourteen hundred and ninety-two, Columbus sailed the ocean blue'), acronyms (such as 'ROY G. BIV' for the colours of the rainbow), acrostics (a verse in which the first letters correspond with the material that needs to be remembered, as in 'Richard Of York Gave Battle In Vain' for the colours of the rainbow) and association ('my PAL the princiPAL' to distinguish its spelling from 'principLE as a ruLE'). Taking each verbal mnemonic technique at a time, consider why they are effective for remembering material.

5 In connection with the above, the World Memory Championship began 'with the host asking the audience to list the eight planets in orbit around the sun in their correct order'. From closest to furthest, the planets are: Mercury, Venus, Earth, Mars, Jupiter, Saturn, Uranus, Neptune and Pluto. Can you devise a verbal mnemonic technique to remember this fact? Do you think that mnemonic devices which people generate themselves are more effective than using those which already exist, and if so, why?

6 Another type of mnemonic method comprises both a verbal and a visual process and is called the 'key' or 'link' word method (note that since it is neither a 'system' nor a 'technique' *per se*, the word 'method' has been used). First systematically studied by Atkinson (1975), the method has been extensively used in the teaching of foreign languages (e.g. Gruneberg, 1992).

The method involves initially constructing a concrete link word or words to represent the foreign word to be learned. For example, the Greek word for 'worm' is 'skooleekee'. This could be represented by two words which sound similar, namely 'school' and 'leaky'. Next, a verbal image is formed connecting the link word or words with its English meaning. For example, the learner could picture his/her school leaky and worms falling from the roof. Once the image has been fixed, which involves the learner thinking very hard about it for at least 10 seconds, the meaning of the Greek word can be obtained by retrieving the key words 'school' and 'leaky' and then the stored image that links these words to 'worm'.

The key or link word method appears to be highly effective as a mnemonic method for learning a foreign language (e.g. Young, 1971). How could a medical student use the method to store the names of the following cranial nerves: olfactory, optic, oculomotor, trochlear, trigeminal, abducens, facial, auditory, glossopharyngeal, vagus, spinal accessory, and hypoglossal? For what other students and in what other situations could the method be usefully employed?

7 Whilst acknowledging it to be 'a useless task', Baddeley (1986) illustrates a mnemonic device for remembering the value of pi (π) to the first 20 decimal places. This involves learning a poem, the number of letters in each word corresponding to a decimal place:

> PIE. I wish I could determine pi
> Eureka cried the great inventor
> Christmas pudding Christmas pie
> Is the Problem's very centre.

The article suggests that Hideaki Tomoyori has bettered Baddeley by some 39 980 places. Do you think Tomoyori employed Baddeley's mnemonic device and, if not, what do you think he would have used? Why do you think people like Tomoyori, Mr Carvello (the man who apparently mastered 24 000 names and numbers from the Cleveland area telephone directory), and Dominic O'Brien (who holds the record for recalling the exact sequence of 25 packs of playing cards) 'would want to absorb a breathtaking quantity of more or less useless information'? Do you think it is, as the article suggests, 'socially painful [and] personally embarrassing' to have a poor memory?

8 Skilled chess players (like David Norwood in the article) can play several games simultaneously, whilst blindfolded, remembering the position of each piece on the various boards (de Groot, 1966). Similarly, expert bridge players have fantastic recall for bridge hands, a feat not dissimilar from that demonstrated by Dominic O'Brien. How do you think such feats can be achieved? It has been shown that if chess pieces are randomly arranged on a board, a skilled player's recall is no better than that of a novice. Does this finding influence how you think such feats are achieved?

References and further reading

Those references which are particularly worthy of further reading are indicated thus: *, together with a brief description of their area of concern.

Atkinson, R.C. (1975) 'Mnemotechnics in second-language learning', *American Psychologist*, 39, pp. 821–8.

*Baddeley, A.D. (1986) *Your Memory: A User's Guide*, Harmondsworth: Penguin. *Written in a clear style, this is one of the more accessible books on human memory.*

Belezza, F.S. (1981) 'Mnemonic Devices: classification, characteristics and criteria', *Review of Educational Research*, 51, pp. 247–75.

Bower, G.H. & Clark, M.C. (1969) 'Narrative stories as mediators for verbal learning', *Psychonomic Science*, 14, pp. 181–2.

Carlson, N.R. (1988) *Discovering Psychology*, London: Allyn & Bacon.

Cermak, L. (1978) *Improving Your Memory*, New York: McGraw-Hill.

de Groot, A. (1966) 'Perception and memory versus thought: some old ideas and recent findings', **in** B. Kleinmontz (Ed.), *Problem Solving*, New York: Wiley.

Gruneberg, M. (1992) *Linkword Language System: Greek*, London: Corgi Books.

Hunter, I.M.L. (1957) *Memory, Facts and Fallacies*, Harmondsworth: Penguin.

*Higbee, K.L. (1989) *Your Memory: How it Works and How to Improve it*, London: Piatkus. *An excellent and very readable guide to the various memory improvement techniques.*

Lorayne, H. & Lucas, J. (1974) *The Memory Book*, Briarcliff Manor, N.Y.: Stein & Day.

*Luria, A.R. (1968) *The Mind of a Mnemonist*, New York: Basic Books. *A dramatic account of the fantastic abilities displayed by 'S'.*

*Paivio, A. (1971/1979) *Imagery and Verbal Processes*, New York: Holt, Rinehart & Winston, and Hillsdale, N.J.: Earlbaum. *A detailed review of the experimental research on imagery.*

Snowman, J., Krebs, E.V. & Lockhart, L. (1980) 'Improving information of recall from prose in high-risk students through Learning Strategy Training', *Journal of Instructional Psychology*, 7, pp. 35–40.

*Yates, E. (1966) *The Art of Memory*, London: Routledge & Kegan Paul. *Provides a classic account of mnemonic devices as well as a history of their use.*

Yesavage, J.A. & Rose, T.L. (1984) 'Semantic elaboration and the method of loci: a new trip for old learners', *Experimental Aging Research*, 10, pp. 155–60.

Young, C.V. (1971) *The Magic of a Mighty Memory*, West Nyack, N.Y.: Parker Publishing Company.